STRANGER
FICTI

C000157868

BEING TALES FROM THE BYWAYS OF
GHOSTS AND FOLK-LORE

BY

MARY L. LEWES

TO
MY SISTER

PREFACE

I HAVE to thank the Editor of the *Occult
Review* for his kindness in allowing me to
reprint here many stories which have appeared
at different times in his magazine.
And I am most grateful to the friends who
have helped to swell the contents of this little
volume, by permitting me to record their
interesting experiences of the supernatural, or
by furnishing me with details concerning local
beliefs and superstitions, which would otherwise have been difficult to obtain.

M. L. LEWES

CONTENTS

CHAPTER I

INTRODUCTORY

"Strange, is it not? that of the myriads who
Before us passed the door of Darkness through,
Not one returns to tell us of the Road,
Which to discover we must travel too."

IF we may judge by the assertion contained in the above quatrain, Omar Khayyám was no believer in ghosts. In which respect the Persian poet must have differed from the general opinion of his times. For until a very few centuries ago, it was only a small minority of those who considered themselves wise above their fellows, who ventured to deny the possibility of the spirit's return to earth. Even amongst the Romans during the Antonine Age (A.D. 98–180), when scepticism on religious matters had become almost universal among the learned, and the worship of the gods had sunk to mere outward observance of ceremony, Gibbon says, "I do not pretend to assert that in this irreligious age, the natural terrors of superstitions, dreams, omens, apparitions, &c., had lost their efficacy." The younger Pliny, in a letter to his friend Sura, writes: " I am extremely desirous to know whether you

1   A

believe in the existence of ghosts, and that they have a real form, and are a sort of divinities, or only the visionary impression of a terrified imagination." He also relates a really exciting tale of a haunted house at Athens, but it is too long to quote here.

The ancients believed that every one possessed three distinct ghosts; the *manes*, of which the ultimate destination was the lower regions, the *spiritus*, which returned to Heaven, and the *umbra*, that, unwilling to sever finally its connection with this life, was wont to haunt the last resting-place of the earthly body. These " shades " were supposed to " walk " between the hours of midnight and cock-crow, causing burial-grounds, cemeteries or tombs to be carefully avoided at night. One reason given as to why very old yew-trees are so often found in country churchyards is, that originally these trees were planted to supply the peasants with wood for their bows, for in lawless times it was soon discovered that the only place where the trees would be safe from nightly marauders was the churchyard, where not the most hardened thief dared venture between darkness and dawn. Particularly were the shades of those who, perishing by crimes of violence without absolution—

" Unhousel'd, disappointed, unanel'd—"

supposed to be uneasy; haunting sometimes the scene of their end, or, in other cases, the footsteps of the slayer. If a living person could summon courage to address one of these haunting spirits (for no ghost may speak unless spoken to) and discover the cause of its restlessness, it was thought possible to give it peace or "lay it," by righting the wrong it suffered from ; whether by vengeance on a murderer, atonement for a crime committed, or by the offices of a priest to give absolution to an unshrived soul. An old writer tells us : "The mode of addressing a Ghost is by commanding it in the name of the three Persons of the Trinity to tell you what it is, and what its business. . . . During the narration of its business a Ghost must by no means be interrupted by questions of any kind ; so doing is extremely dangerous. . . ."

Besides believing in these ghosts of departed human beings, there was ever present in the minds of our forefathers, the dread of a host of "evil spirits" who were the agents and assistants of Satan, always ready to injure innocent souls, and where possible, to cause worldly disaster also. Magicians and sorcerers * were supposed by their arts to have power in this world of demons, the forfeit being their own souls, lost beyond redemption. In his delightful "Memoirs," Benvenuto Cellini (1500–1571) describes with great vividness some experiments he conducted with a necromancer at Rome, in order to discover the whereabouts of a girl he

---

* Magicians were able to command spirits to do their bidding, while sorcerers, though they could *summon* demons, were obliged to obey them.

loved. The magician was a Sicilian priest, "a man of genius and well versed in the Latin and Greek authors," who made an appointment with Cellini for a certain evening, desiring him to bring two companions. "I invited Vincenzo Romoli . . . he brought with him a native of Pistoja, who cultivated the black art himself." The trio then repaired to the Colosseum, where the priest ". . . began to draw circles upon the ground with the most impressive ceremonies imaginable. . . ." After this sort of thing and many incantations had lasted an hour and a half, "there appeared several legions of devils, insomuch that the amphitheatre was quite filled with them." This terrible phenomenon sounds dreadful enough to have frightened most people, but obtaining no result from his inquiries on the first occasion, Cellini was intrepid enough to arrange for a second experiment, his account of which absolutely bristles with demons and bad spirits; the strange part being that he writes as if their appearance at the sorcerer's bidding was the most natural thing in the world, and quite what he had expected to see. And this attitude of absolute, matter-of-fact faith in the powers of darkness, and acceptance of the magician's arts, is very interesting in the man, of whose famous autobiography John Addington Symonds wrote : "The Genius of the Renaissance, incarnate in a single personality, leans forth and speaks to us."

It is only when we begin to investigate the

origin of certain old customs and superstitions
that we gain any real idea of how deeply rooted
in men's minds during the Dark and Middle
Ages was the fear of the supernatural, and
particularly of evil spirits. To this day in
Pembrokeshire, the cottagers, after the Satur-
day morning scrubbing, take a piece of chalk
and draw a rough geometrical pattern round
the edge of the threshold stone. This they
do, not knowing that their ancestors thought
it a sure way of keeping the Devil from
entering the house. Another custom, often
noticeable in country parishes, is the reluctance
to bury the dead on the north side of the
churchyard; this is because evil spirits were
always supposed to lurk on that side of the
church precincts.

For many centuries Christianity, at all
events among the mass of the people, seemed
powerless to raise the dark veil of superstition
which the old pagan beliefs had spread over
the world; and indeed in many countries—
sometimes from ignorance, sometimes from
motives of expediency—heathen traditions and
practices were preserved, and merely trans-
ferred to a Christian setting. Particularly was
this the case among the Celtic nations, whose
Christianity must in the early ages have merely
been grafted on the native Druid beliefs. For
the material that the great Irish and Welsh
missionaries had to work with was rough
indeed; and any drastic attempt to impose
a new system of religion on a horde of Celtic

tribesmen would doubtless have ended in speedy disaster. So it is probable that St. Patrick and St. David and their evangelist successors, instead of bluntly denouncing the most cherished of the heathen legends, merely took and adapted them to their own teaching; giving them first a decent Christian garb. Two instances of evident adaptation are quoted by Mr. Elworthy, in his book "The History of the Evil Eye," where he remarks : " Here in Britain the goddess of love was turned into St. Brychan's daughter ; and as late as the fourteenth century lovers are said to have come from all parts to pray at her shrine in Anglesey. Another similar example is found in the confusion of St. Bridget and an Irish goddess, whose gifts were poetry, fire and medicine . . . almost all the incidents in her legend can be referred to the Pagan ritual."

And though so many long centuries have passed since the days when the Druid priests offered propitiatory sacrifices to the spirits that dwelt in the great oak-trees, yet in the minds of the descendants of those old Celts (in spite of all that civilisation and intermixture with other races have done) there still lingers a trace of mystery, a readiness of belief in things outside the realm of the five senses, which perhaps future ages will never quite obliterate. For this quality, call it what we will (and too often it has degenerated into mere superstition), is yet of the " Unknown," and for all we can tell may indeed be a spark, though dwindled, of the Divine fire. As every one knows, among the Highlanders this curious mystic vein sometimes produces seers, and their gift is called "second sight." According to a very interesting book called "A Description of the Western Islands of Scotland," published in 1703, this power of foretelling the future was in those days a recognised talent possessed by certain individuals, which apparently excited but little surprise among the rest of the community. The writer of the "Description" says: "It is an ordinary thing for them (the seers) to see a Man who is to come to the house shortly after, and if he is not of the Seer's acquaintance, yet he gives such a lively description of his Stature, Complexion, Habit, &c., that upon his arrival he answers the character given him in all respects. I have been seen thus myself by Seers of both sexes at some hundred miles' distance—some that saw me in this manner had never seen me personally." In Wales also, if we may believe the old writers, there seems to have been a class of persons somewhat resembling the Highland seers, and called "Awenyddion" (inspired people). "When consulted upon any doubtful event, they roar out violently, and become as it were possessed of an evil spirit. They deliver the answer in sentences that are trifling, and have little meaning, but are elegantly expressed. In the meantime, he who watches what is said unriddles the answer from some turn of a word. They are then roused as from a deep sleep,

and by violent shaking compelled to return
to their senses, when they lose all recollection
of the answers they gave."

And though the day of the Awenyddion is
long past, yet something of their inspiration,
and a faint echo of the bards' songs of valour
and enchantments seems still to linger about
the mountains of Wales. It is true that down
in the valleys the railways and Council schools
have routed the " Tylwyth Teg " (fairies) from
those " sweet green fields " of which Matthew
Arnold wrote ; and the young generation has
no time to spare for listening in the winter
evenings to the old folks' tales of haunted
" mansions," or of the " canwyll corph," or the
awe-inspiring " Gŵrach " spectre. And there
are very few people left now who will mistake
the weird cry of a string of wild geese flying
high overhead in the winter dusk, for the
shrieks of tormented souls pursued by the
hounds of hell. Still, though fast disappearing,
some of the old tales and beliefs are not
entirely lost in the more remote localities ;
and it was with the idea of preserving a few
of them from oblivion that this book was
begun. Living, as I have for many years, in
a hitherto little-known part of the Principality,
where almost every old country house has its
ghost (sometimes more than one), and where
the highest hill is crowned by the grave of
a mighty " caŵr " (or giant)—though archæ-
ologists will tell you that it is merely a British
burial-mound—and where the neighbouring

lake is inhabited by fairy cattle that disappear at the approach of man; it is impossible not to feel regretful that all these old stories should be forgotten. Especially will any one feel this who happens to have Celtic blood in his veins; in which case, and if he inhabits a corner of "fair Cambria," some of the things he hears will not appear so highly improbable and far-fetched as they might to the less imaginative Saxon. We all know Owen Glendower's celebrated assertion:

> "I can call spirits from the vasty deep,"

and his description of the wonders that local tradition told him had preceded his birth. And we remember Hotspur's aggravating retort to what he doubtless considered the empty boasting of the great Welshman. But living amongst a people absolutely steeped in occult and legendary lore, quite ready to attribute any extraordinary characteristics in their leaders to supernatural aid, there is little doubt that Glendower's belief in his wizard powers was as entirely sincere as his courage and energy were unquestioned. But one rather sympathises, too, with Hotspur, when he describes afterwards how Glendower had kept him up

> "last night, at least nine hours,
> In reckoning up the several devils' names
> That were his lackeys."

Most people like a good "ghost story." Even the loudest of scoffers does so really; and he is generally the person who draws his chair nearest to that of the story-teller, and who, after asserting that the tale is "all rubbish," will nevertheless proceed to say what he would have done at that particular point in the narrative when "the candle burnt blue, and a faint rattling of chains was heard," &c. &c. But, as a fact, there are few real old-fashioned scoffers left. We have passed through the phase of extreme incredulity regarding occult happenings which was inevitable, and was merely the swing of the pendulum from the rank superstition and ignorance of the Middle Ages. Few people now venture to declare that "there are no such things as ghosts"; for the mass of evidence collected and weighed by savants, such as Gurney, Myers, Hodgson, T. H. Hudson, and Sir Oliver Lodge, is overwhelming as regards the truth that things *have* happened, and do still happen, quite outside the limit of human explanation. But while most intelligent persons admit this, the time is still far distant when we shall be able to say how or why these things occur; though, guided by some of the greatest thinkers of our day, we may at last dare to hope that our feet are set in the path of knowledge, and that at some future time humanity may perhaps reach the goal, and lift the dark and impenetrable curtain that hides the Unseen. Whether the world will be any better off, when, or if, that happens, concerns us of this generation not at all; in fact, most of us who have this world's work to do, will find it best to leave close investigation of supernormal phenomena to those who are able to approach such subjects with a scientific mind, capable of recognising and collecting truthful evidence, and of detecting and setting aside what is false. And how very much the false outweighs the true, when it comes to a question of evidence in psychic inquiry, only the really conscientious searcher knows. All sorts of questions rise up in the mind of the critical inquirer and have to be satisfied before he will admit the impossibility of accounting by human explanation for the experiences brought to his notice. And besides the need for this severely critical attitude of mind, which we do not all of us possess, and in many cases the lack of leisure necessary for such abstract study, there is another reason why it is best for the majority of us to refrain from speculating overmuch on the whys and hows of these glimpses of the "Unknown" that we are occasionally granted. It is because many people have actually not the strength of mind necessary to withstand the possible shock occasioned by occult experiences, and for these, such studies end only too often in mental disaster. This assertion may sound exaggerated, but it is not so; and if it serves as a hint of warning to those over-fond of dabbling in a sea of mystery, fathomless and wide beyond all human imaginings, so much the better.

After these remarks, it will be realised that this book has nothing to do with the scientific aspect of "ghost-hunting," but is merely an attempt to gather together a number of stories dealing with the supernatural, and particularly those connected with the old superstitions and beliefs of Welsh people which have happened to come to my knowledge. Of course some of these tales are absurd, and interesting only from their quaintness; yet in many of them there is an element which, as the French say, "gives to think," and should interest serious students of the occult in search of fresh material. So, much of the ghostly gossip in the following chapters belongs to Wales; indeed my original purpose was to deal with Welsh ghosts and superstitions only. But in the course of collection, I came across so many interesting particulars and incidents concerning people and places beyond the borders of the Principality, that I decided to include them in this volume, on the chance that they may be new to most of my readers. All the stories to be narrated are what are known as "true" ones, or have at least a well-established reputation in tradition; the majority having either been told me at first-hand, or imparted by people who believed in their truth, and who, in many cases, had personal knowledge of the people whose experiences they related, and of the localities they described.

Naturally, such tales as follow, in which hearsay must figure considerably, cannot lay claim to the evidential value possessed by the carefully sifted records of the Psychical Research Society. But it may be pointed out that many of the stories contained in Chapters II., III., and IV. concern the constant *repetition* of certain definite phenomena, a feature which strongly supports belief in their foundation on a basis of truth.

For instance, it seems to happen continually that a person going to a house which he does not know is haunted, sees a " ghost," and afterwards finds, on relating his experience, that the apparition he describes is exactly what other people have also seen. A good example of this occurs in Chapter IV., where " Colonel and Mrs. West " saw the ghost of the headless woman, being previously unaware that they were occupying a haunted room.

This agreement in the testimony of people who at different times, and generally quite unprepared, have seen particular apparitions is an interesting fact in itself, and surely not to be altogether despised as evidence of the cumulative order, though the scientific details demanded by the professional ghost-hunter may be lacking.

The stories in my later chapters dealing with some ancient Welsh superstitions need no comment, as, whatever may be thought of them as supernatural incidents, their interest from the standpoint of folk-lore is indisputable, and for that reason alone they are worth recording.

Throughout this book I shall change the real names of people for fictitious ones or initials, for reasons that will be obvious to every one. There are a few exceptions; and where they occur they will be noted. In most cases I shall disguise the names of houses, and sometimes those of villages and towns; but where the names of counties are mentioned, they are the true ones.

CHAPTER II

WELSH GHOSTS

" A kind of old Hobgoblin Hall
  Now somewhat fallen to decay,
  With weather-stains upon the wall,
  And stairways worn, and crazy doors,
  And creaking and uneven floors,
  And chimneys huge and tiled and tall."

IN one of the most remote parts of South Wales
there stands on a low cliff that is washed by
the waters of a certain bay in St. George's
Channel a very curious old house which we will
call Plâsgwyn. Inside one finds walls many
feet in thickness, dark panelled rooms with
enormous cupboards, and a beautiful oak staircase, its shallow, uneven steps polished by the
feet of many generations. Of course there is a
ghost story too, and one possessing an element
of picturesqueness, its origin dating far back to
the days when smuggling was considered by
quite respectable people as a useful means of
increasing their income in a gentlemanly
manner.

When one reflects on the lonely situation of
Plâsgwyn, and listens—especially in winter—
to the boom of wind and wave advertising with
loud persistence the nearness of the sea, it is

15

not difficult for the imagination to conjure up those far-away times; to picture the landing of many an interesting cargo in the little cove hard by when the nights were dark and stormy and the Revenue men off their guard; and to conjecture that perhaps many crimes were committed at that period by villains using the smuggler's cloak to cover misdoing, and that possibly some such dark deed may have happened in the old house, thus giving a real foundation to our story.

It begins with an incident that was told me as having occurred a few years ago at Plâsgwyn. One day two maidservants went to do some work in the largest bedroom, used always as a visitors' room. When they quickly came downstairs again, with white faces and trembling knees, they had a strange tale to tell. They declared that in the room, floating in the air near the bed, they had seen what appeared to be a human hand and wrist, bleeding as if just severed from an arm, the fingers of the hand covered with splendid rings. Horribly frightened, the two maids did not look long at the apparition but fled downstairs as fast as they could. However, so convinced were they both of the reality of the thing they saw that neither could ever be induced to enter the room alone as long as they remained in the house, and one at least was in the service of the family for some years.

Now the legend of Plâsgwyn is as follows. Long ago a strange lady of great wealth once stayed there, and, for reasons now unknown, her hosts went away leaving her alone one night. Feeling solitary and remembering with alarm tales she had heard of the lawless doings of smugglers known to frequent the coast, she went early to her room and tried to sleep. Well-grounded indeed were her fears, for in the middle of the night she was aroused by loud knocking at her door and rough voices demanding admittance. Terrified, the lady tried to hold the door, but in vain. It soon gave way beneath violent blows, and her arm, thrust forward in feeble resistance, was seized and held. Unfortunately, she had forgotten to remove her rings, of which she wore many of great size and brilliance, and the sight of the jewels so excited the greedy robbers that they immediately tried to pull them off. They fitted the fingers so tightly, however, that they would not move; accordingly, the ruffians, determined to have possession of them, ruthlessly chopped off the poor woman's hand and wrist, immediately afterwards decamping with their dreadful booty. Ever since that night, runs the tale, those who have the " gift " may sometimes see the jewel-covered hand hovering over the bed in the room once occupied by the ill-fated lady.

Nor is the spectral hand the only uncanny thing to be seen at Plâsgwyn, if local rumour be correct; which declares that the spirit of " Old Brown," a former owner of the property, and from all accounts a person of much

B

character (whether good or bad matters not), has been seen in a ball of fire rolling down the staircase into the hall at midnight !

I have never met anybody who has witnessed this somewhat alarming phenomenon, but the legend is merely related for what it is worth, and as it was told me by a very old inhabitant of the neighbourhood. And whether the " ball of fire " is only an absurdity, originating in some one's too lively imagination, or really one of those " fire elementals " of which advanced occultists tell us, must be left to the reader's judgment to determine. But there are few people of imagination who could visit this quaint old house without feeling that scarcely any tale of the marvellous relating to it would sound incredible in such a setting.

Of quite a different type is another incident connected with the same place, which, though it certainly lacks sensation, is curious as one of that class of apparently pointless events so realistic as to seem commonplace, and which yet leave one in a perfect " cul-de-sac " of mystification as to why they should have happened at all.

Many years ago—perhaps thirty or forty—a meet of the hounds took place at Plâsgwyn. Most of the houses round sent representatives, but the meet was not a large one. Among those who drove over were a Mrs. A. and her friend Miss B. When riders and hounds had trotted off to draw the coverts near the house, the hostess, Mrs. C., suggested that she and her daughter, with Mrs. A. and her friend, should walk out and watch the find. The two elder ladies kept on the main road, just outside the drive gate, while Miss C. and Miss B., more energetic, went through some fields and climbed a little hill which commanded a good view of the covert where the hounds were. Just beneath them was the field where all the riders were grouped, and beyond that was the road, a short stretch of which was plainly visible from the hill, though at each end of this open piece it was hidden by the trees.

After they had been waiting some little time on the hill-side, the two ladies heard the sound of a horse trotting quietly along the road beneath the trees, and very soon a rider mounted on a white horse, and wearing a red coat, emerged in the open part of the road, presently disappearing again beneath the further trees.

Miss B. remarked : "That must be Mr. X." (the only gentleman in the district who usually hunted on a white horse), "how late he is." And she and Miss C. concluded that Mr. X. was making his way down the road to where a gate beyond the trees would take him into the field where the rest of the hunters were gathered. But the minutes passed, and he never came to join the other riders, though Miss B. and her friend must have seen him if he had done so. However, they supposed that he was perhaps waiting in the road after all, hidden by the trees, and so thought no more of the matter.

Later on when the ladies were lunching at Plâsgwyn, and were joined by some of the returned hunters, Miss B. mentioned having seen Mr. X. go along the road towards the covert. "You must be mistaken," said one of the party, "he was not out to-day." The two ladies then described the rider they had seen, and were still more puzzled when told that *no one* had appeared with the hounds wearing a red coat and riding a white horse! Yet Miss B. and her friend knew they had both seen such a horseman, and that he was as absolutely real to them as the rest of the "field" close by. The odd thing was, that a good many people were gathered in the road beneath the trees behind the open stretch referred to, among them being Mrs. A. and Mrs. C. Now none of these people had seen any such rider pass them, though he was coming from their direction when he became visible to Miss B. on the hill, and yet he must have been a noticeable figure in his red coat on the white horse. He certainly did not come from the opposite direction and then turn in his tracks before reaching the foot-people, because in that case he must have been seen arriving by Miss B. and Miss C. who had been waiting some time on the hill-side overlooking the road. The mystery was never solved, for when Miss B. next saw Miss C. the latter said she had made inquiries amongst other people who were out hunting that day, and no one had seen the man on the white horse. Neither had he been seen by the country people, though as is usual in Wales on a hunting day, there were a good many labourers, &c., round the coverts and in the fields, snatching an

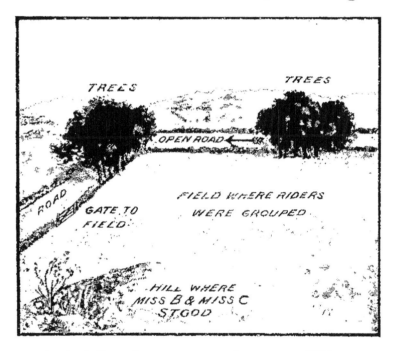

hour's holiday for a taste of sport. When relating the experience to me after the lapse of many years, Miss B. said she had no theory to offer on the subject, having always regarded it as a mystery defying ordinary explanation.

There does not seem to be any tradition connected with Plâsgwyn which would throw light on the appearance of this phantom horseman, but a short time ago, I thought I had really come across his track, in conversation with a certain friend. This Mr. R. declared that once when he and others were hunting on the hills, they suddenly saw an "unknown horseman" riding with the hounds, who, as they approached him, disappeared, no one knew whither, nobody at the time or since having been able to "place" him, either as a stranger or inhabitant of the country. But that the apparition *was* an apparition, and no horse or man of flesh and blood, Mr. R. seemed firmly persuaded. Roughly speaking, the district where this mysterious rider was seen would be about a dozen miles from Plâsgwyn.

But there are two phantom hunt legends belonging to Cardiganshire. Of one I have only gleaned the very vaguest particulars, to the effect that on a certain farm in the seaboard parish of Penbryn, a ghostly pack of hounds and hunters have occasionally been seen, all circumstantial details, or any origin for the tale being wanting.

The other tradition of a spectral chase is really picturesque, and located in the neighbourhood of the little town of Lland——l, is related by Mr. Alfred Rees, in his charming book "Ianto the Fisherman." Condensed, the story runs that long ago there lived, a few miles from Lland——l, an old gentleman-farmer, who was well known and liked as a true sportsman throughout the county. He kept a pack of harriers, and had hunting

rights over a considerable tract of country.
His end was tragic, for one November evening,
when returning late with the hounds, he was
shot in the woods above the house by a
supposed poacher ; though in spite of the great
hue and cry raised by such a foul deed, the
murderer managed to evade justice. But,
"the villagers still declare, that whenever
November nights are moonlit and windy, the
huntsman's horn is heard above the wood, and
the pack winds down the glade in full music,
till suddenly a shot echoes in the valley, after
which there is silence. They declare that Will
the Saddler, a sober deacon, coming home
one night, when he had taken some mended
harness to a farmer at the top of the wood,
witnessed plainly a full repetition of the
tragedy. The opening scene appeared so real,
that unmindful of religious prejudices, he
actually joined in the chase, till with the flash
of the gun he remembered the story, and
presently saw shadowy forms, attended by
hounds and horse, pass by him down the glade
with muttered whisperings, bearing the burden
of their dead."

Another phantom horseman figures in the
tradition attached to an old and well-known
Welsh house ; which says, that always before
a death occurs in the family, a noise of galloping
hoofs is heard coming up the drive towards
the house at dead of night. Nearer and nearer
it draws, passing at length under the windows,
then ceases suddenly at the front door, as if a

horse were violently reined in there. A pause succeeds, then loud hoof-beats again, hurry-scurry past the windows, and so down the drive, growing ever fainter, till they are lost in distance. If sleepers are awakened and rush to look out, nothing can be seen. But in the morning, fresh hoof-marks will be found upon the gravel.*

Mention of these ghostly horses and riders reminds one that Pembrokeshire—in common with several other districts in Great Britain and Ireland—possesses a good phantom coach legend, localised in the southern part of the county, at a place where four roads meet, called Sampson Cross. In old days, the belated farmer, driving home in his gig from market, was apt to cast a nervous glance over his shoulder as his pony slowly climbed the last steep pitch leading up to the Cross. For he remembered the story connected with that dark bit of road, that told how every night a certain Lady Z. (who lived in the seventeenth century, and whose monument is in the church close by) drives over from Tenby, ten miles distant, in a coach drawn by headless horses, guided by a headless coachman. She also has

* The noise of a ghostly equipage being driven to the door is to be heard at Ô—l T—e, a house in Ireland. A friend who lived there for some months told me she heard it not once but several times, and not only she, but other people in the house heard it also. The sound was described as unmistakably that of heavy carriage wheels; yet nothing was to be *seen*, nor could such a characteristic noise be accounted for in any other way.

no head ; and arriving by midnight at Sampson Cross, the whole equipage is said to disappear in a flame of fire, with a loud noise of explosion. A clergyman living in the immediate neighbour-hood, who told me the story, said that some people believed the ghostly traveller had been safely "laid" many years ago, in the waters of a lake not far distant. He added, however that might be, it was an odd fact that his sedate and elderly cob, when driven past the Cross after nightfall, would invariably start as if frightened there, a thing which never happened by daylight.

It is not every one who is acquainted with the precise meaning of the expression "laying a ghost," which Brand in his "Antiquities" advises as the best remedy for cases of troublesome hauntings. "Sometimes," he says, "Ghosts appear and disturb a house without deigning to give a reason for so doing ; with these the shortest way is to lay them. For this purpose there must be two or three clergymen and the ceremony must be performed in Latin. . . . A Ghost may be laid for any time less than a hundred years and in any place or body, as a solid oak, the point of a sword, or a barrel of beer, or a pipe of wine. . . . But of all places the most common and what a ghost least likes is the Red Sea." From another authority we learn that seven parsons are necessary to this weird performance. They must all sit in a row, each holding a lighted candle, and should all seven candles continue to burn steadily, it shows that not one of the reverend gentlemen is capable of wrestling with the uneasy spirit. But if one of the lights suddenly goes out, it is a sign that its holder may read the prayers of exorcism, though in so doing he must be careful that the ghost (who will mockingly repeat the words) does not get a line ahead of him. If this happens his labour is lost, and the ghost will defy his efforts and remain a wanderer. In some parts of the country it was believed that only a Roman Catholic priest could lay a ghost successfully.

But to return to Pembrokeshire. About a mile or so from Sampson Cross, there is a certain rectory said to be haunted by a mysterious " grey figure " which sometimes showed itself in the " best bedroom." Two visitors, on different occasions (having previously known nothing of any supposed ghost in the house), declared that they had seen a " grey lady " standing by their bedside. A daughter of the house, who told me about this apparition, added that though she herself had never *seen* anything, yet one night when she chanced to sleep in this room, she had been awakened by the most horrible and mysterious noises. She described the sounds as resembling " the groans and cries of a tortured animal," and they came, not from beneath the window (which looked on a strip of garden), but apparently from high up in the air above it, and could not be accounted for in any ordinary way. Nor does there seem to be any story connected with the house in past times which might afford a clue to the meaning of these hauntings ; or if any event of tragic or dramatic significance ever took place there, it has been forgotten by the present generation. Yet it is quite reasonable to suppose that some such event may have happened at that lonely rectory. There must be few houses, constantly inhabited for, let us say, fifty years, of which the walls have not witnessed many varying circumstances of life—circumstances of joy and woe, and all the shades between. And besides actual events, think of the developments of human character, the play of different temperaments, and the range of passions and emotions that any such house has sheltered ! And if, as some psychologists aver, human passions, thoughts, and emotions have at their greatest height actual dynamic force, capable of leaving impressions on their environment which may endure for ages, and even be perceptible to certain people— then does not this assertion supply us with a reason for many of the unexplained " ghosts " and hauntings of which one so constantly hears ?

For we can easily believe that these impressions would be most apt to linger round those earthly scenes best known in life, and where perhaps only the most ordinary chain of familiar events sufficed to lead up to the crisis which evoked the elemental passions and emotional force of some strong personality.

Certainly the lady who furnished the few particulars about the rectory ghost must possess the sixth sense necessary for the perception of these impressions, for she added that she had once seen an apparition in another Pembrokeshire house, where she happened to be staying. One day during her visit, as she was coming out of her room in search of a book she wanted from the bookcase on the landing, she suddenly saw a woman's figure appear in front of her. "A little thin person," she described, "dressed in light blue, with sandy hair, much dragged up on top of her head," presenting altogether such a curious old-fashioned appearance that Miss L——d looked very hard at her, and wondered who she could be, and where she had appeared from. But the next moment the figure vanished from view through the door of another bedroom. Although her curiosity was rather roused by the odd looks of the woman she had seen, Miss L——d thought little of the incident, imagining she must have seen one of the servants in rather strange attire. And it was only when she had been several days longer in the house that she discovered it possessed no inmate in the slightest degree resembling the queer apparition of the landing, which she was forced to conclude was no human being, but most probably the family ghost ! Personally I know this house well, and had always heard there was supposed to be a ghost there ; but though I have often stayed there, and even slept in the

" haunted " room, I never saw the sandy-haired lady, nor anything else of an uncanny nature.

In fact, the county of Pembroke is a happy hunting-ground for the ghost-tracker. Nor is this to be wondered at, considering the innumerable associations, legendary, historical and romantic connected with a tract of country which is certainly one of the most interesting in Great Britain. So that the student of ghost-lore and superstition will there discover a fine field for research, the only pity being that in Pembrokeshire as in other parts of Wales, although almost every other old country house has its ghost, yet the stories and legends connected with these apparitions and hauntings are very often forgotten, and only vague details as to " noises," or doubtful reports of spectral appearances are forthcoming. However, in the case of one house (which we will call Hill-view), some kind of explanation is given of hauntings which seem to have continued for a long time, and have been remarked by various people who have rented the place. I first heard of the Hill-view ghost many years ago, when it was said to have caused a frightful noise one night in a room upstairs, which was apparently reserved for visitors, and at the time that the sound was heard was unoccupied. The noise was described as exactly like the thud and crash that a large piece of furniture, such as a wardrobe, would make in falling heavily on the floor;

there seemed no mistaking the sound for anything else. Yet when with fear and trembling
the door was opened, those who looked in were
astonished to find nothing unusual in the empty
room, or in the dressing-room which opened off
it. All was in order, darkness, and silence,
and search as they would, nothing that could
possibly account for such a noise could be
found, nor was the problem ever solved. That
happened a long while ago, but quite lately,
the present occupants of the house were one
day sitting in the room immediately beneath
the bedroom before referred to, when they
distinctly saw the door open, apparently of
itself, and heard a sound as of some one entering
the room. On another occasion also, members
of the family have heard mysterious footsteps;
but none of them seem to have heeded the
ghost very much until a certain friend came to
stay with them. This friend they put to sleep
in the haunted bedroom, and one night spent
there seems to have been quite enough for her.
Next morning she complained that she could
get no sleep, owing to the incessant noises—
knockings, rappings, and scrapings—which went
on all night.

That something of a sinister nature may still
linger about that room is not strange, if local
report be true; which says that a very long
time ago a little boy—a son of the family who
owned the property—was dreadfully ill-treated
by a nurse or governess, and shut up in a
cupboard in the room now haunted, where

the poor child was eventually discovered, dead.

Not a thousand miles from Hill-view is a house (we will temporarily christen it Shipton Rise) which possesses a rather interesting little story connected with a picture that hangs in the dining-room representing a ship, called the *Shipton Rise*. The original of this picture was a vessel commanded once upon a time by one Captain Joseph Turner, of the East India Company's service. During a long voyage on this ship, he was one night awakened by a voice, which said, "Joseph Turner, get up and sound the well." He thought he was dreaming, and promptly went to sleep again. A second time the same call woke him, and again he paid no attention, and slept. But once more came the voice, more insistent than before, "Joseph Turner, Joseph Turner, sound the well!" This time he was really roused, and felt so impressed that he determined to do as he was bid. So he went, and sounded the ship's well, and found a great leak sprung. The pumps were manned, and thanks to the timely warning, the ship was saved.

It is extraordinary how very many stories of occult occurrences belong to what we may call the "warning type"; yet among them we find few resembling the foregoing instance, in which the message conveyed by ghostly voice or visitant has been of use in averting misfortune. In fact these supernormal intimations seem to be generally heralds of the inevitable, rather than friendly envoys of any special Providence. The traditional " White Swans of Closeburn "; the mysterious " Drummer-boy " of the Airlies; the Lytteltons' " White Lady " (all figuring in tales too well known for repetition), belong to this very large class of supernatural incident which it seems only impending calamity can evoke.

In this connection there is a rather curious sequel added to the "family ghost" story of Mayfield, a very old house in West Wales, dating back to the year 1600. Among the family portraits there, one is shown the picture of a young lady in the dress of the eighteenth century. This was a Mrs. Jones (Jones shall replace the real name of the family) and an ancestress of the present owner of the house. Tradition says that a wicked butler murdered this poor lady 'n a large cupboard—almost a little room—which opens out of the dining-room. He then fled with the family plate, but finding it too heavy, he dropped part of his plunder in a ditch near the house, where it was subsequently found, though history is silent as regards the fate of the butler. Ever since then, the ghost of the murdered lady walks out of the cupboard every Christmas evening (the anniversary of the tragedy), never appearing till the ladies have left the dinner-table. At least, so runs the tale; and now for the sequel.

Early in the last century, Mayfield and the property were owned by a certain Jones, who had a brother living in India. Whether Mr.

Jones was a bachelor or widower at the time of the following occurrence, one does not know, but at all events he lived at Mayfield by himself. He used the dining-room as a sitting-room of an evening, and after his dinner would turn his chair round to the fire, and sit there reading till it was bed-time. One night he had sat up later than usual, and as he shut up his book and bethought him of bed, the clock struck midnight. In the corner of the room, behind his chair, was the cupboard already referred to. Now as the last stroke of twelve died away, Mr. Jones heard the click of the door opening. He turned his head and there, walking out of the cupboard towards him, he saw the figure of a woman dressed in an old-fashioned costume. She advanced a few paces, stopped, and said in loud, clear tones, "Your brother is dead." Then she turned and walked back into the cupboard, the door of which shut with a loud clang. As soon as he recovered from his astonishment, Mr. Jones made a thorough search of the cupboard and room, but could find no trace of any inmate. Convinced at length that a message from the other world had been brought to him, he made a careful note of the date and hour of the incident. In those days letters took a long while to travel from India to this country, and he had therefore many weeks to wait before the mail brought him news that his brother had died, the time of death *coinciding exactly* with the night and hour in

c

which he was warned by the apparition at Mayfield.

Another incident which seems to have fore-shadowed death (though the warning in this case was not definitely given) recurs to my mind, and though trivial in a way, it yet possesses a certain impressiveness, perhaps from its very simplicity and lack of any dramatic element. Or perhaps it is only because the locality described is so familiar to me that the following little story seems more weird and realistic than it really is. The reader must imagine one of the most peaceful and beautiful spots in Wales, where there stands a large, square house called Wernafon, backed by hanging oak woods, beneath which flows a clear river. Higher up the vale the stream loiters through pleasant meadows, afford-ing the angler many a tempting pool; but as it reaches Wernafon, it begins to sing and clatter over stone and shingle as if it already heard the calling of the not far-distant sea, while in flood-time, heavy water rushes down, deeply covering stepping-stones, and swamp-ing shallow fords. So, for the convenience of the Wernafon workmen and labourers, and others who live on the hither side of the river, it is spanned near the house by a narrow, wooden foot-bridge, which saves people a con-siderable walk round.

Many years ago, there lived on the Wernafon estate, two labourers, whom we will call Ben and Tom; and these men were great friends.

They had worked together from boyhood, and when at last—both being old—Ben died, Tom felt sadly lonely and forlorn. One day, soon after his friend's funeral, he had occasion to cross the river by the little foot-bridge, and as he trudged heavily along its narrow planks, his head bent down in melancholy thought, he suddenly came to a full stop, for there was a man standing in the middle of the bridge. Moreover, as he looked hard at the man, he somehow became aware that it was Ben who stood there, and who smiled at Tom as if glad to see him. Entirely forgetting for the moment that he had seen Ben buried but a few days before, Tom accosted him, and a short conversation ensued between the two about ordinary, every-day matters. But suddenly Ben asked his friend "if he would like to see the inside of Wernafon, for," said he, "I go there every night, and a strange sight it is to see the people all asleep while I pass through." He then offered to take Tom through the house that very night, if he would meet him again on the bridge at midnight; and without waiting for an answer, he glided along the bridge, and disappeared. Immediately and with a feeling of horror, it dawned on Tom that the man he had just talked to had actually been dead for several days, and he began to think he had seen a vision or had had some extraordinary dream. Nevertheless, being a courageous old fellow, and at the same time curious to see if any result would follow, he determined to keep the strange appointment. So midnight found him waiting on the little bridge. A bright moon illumined the river and banks, and by its soft light, the old workman was presently aware of a dark shape hastening to join him. Greeting the living man, the apparition took his former comrade by the hand, and led him to the front door of Wernafou, which, as might be expected, was closely locked and barred. But at a touch from Tom's escort, the great door opened without a sound, and the companions passed into the hall of the house. There, the silence of sleep and complete darkness reigned. Yet without a stumble, Tom found himself mounting the staircase with his ghostly guide. Arrived on the landing, the pair stopped before a closed door, which immediately opened, allowing them to enter. Softly they crept into the room, Tom remarking that it seemed filled with a faint bluish light, unlike anything he had ever seen before. They gazed at the occupant of the room wrapped in deep slumber, and creeping out again, visited all the other rooms in turn, Tom becoming more and more bewildered by the strangeness of his experience. At last—how he hardly knew— he found himself standing again in the moonlight outside the front door; and turning to speak to his friend, discovered that he was alone. He rubbed his eyes in astonishment, for an instant before, Ben had been standing by his side. And now, except the fact of finding.

himself in such an unusual place at so late an hour, nothing remained to show that his adventure had been real and not a dream. He went home, wondering greatly at what had happened, and it does not appear that he saw the apparition again before his death, which occurred suddenly, only a few days after his mysterious experience.

At a much later period than the date of the above story, but still some years ago, a curious instance of the "warning" kind occurred at N——e, which is a hamlet distant a few miles from Wernafon. Though in this case there is nothing tragic or of an important character to record, yet it is worth recounting on the ground of coincidence alone, if coincidence it really was.

About eight o'clock one summer evening, several neighbours happened to be at the blacksmith's house, having a quiet smoke and gossip together. They were sitting in a room at the back of the smithy, which faced the main road. Suddenly the talkers in this room were startled by the sound of a tremendous crash. Exclaiming "Some one's cart must have upset on the road," they all rushed out through the shop, fully expecting to see some bad accident. To every one's surprise, all was still, the road empty, and no sign of any vehicle could be seen in either direction. Much perplexed, they went home, but the next evening, most of them were again at the smith's, and of course began to discuss

the strange incident of the night before. But
as the clock struck eight, again came the same
terrific noise. Once more they ran out, and
this time they found a heavily laden cart
upset on the road just outside the forge.

Nobody seems to have been killed or even
hurt by the accident, and one wonders why, in
the case of such an—apparently—unimportant
event, such an impressive and collective warning should have been given.

Among my notes, I find mention of a little
house near this same village of N——e, which
was reputed to be haunted. The note says :
" Mr. Z. (an old gentleman well versed in the
antiquities and folk-lore of his district) told
me about a haunted house called Tyhir. . . .
About twenty years ago, the man who lived
there used to see *curious, little people*, of the
size that could run under a chair, walking
about the house. This man was so nervous of
what he heard and saw that he would never,
if he could help it, stay alone in the house.
Mr. Z. spoke once to another man, who had
often gone to keep the other company on
Sundays, when he was afraid to sit in the
house by himself. This second man told
Mr. Z. that though he himself had seen
nothing, yet he had heard noises which were
quite unaccountable. The 'little people' seen
were said to exactly resemble in feature the
former dwellers in the house ; a little old man
called ' Tom Tyhir,' and his wife."

Cases of apparitions that have acted as

protectors in danger to the percipient are
occasionally heard of, and one of the most
interesting stories of this type was recorded in
a well-known Welsh newspaper, about two
years ago, and will quite bear repetition in these
pages. To quote the original words : " A story
which appears strange even in these days of
telepathic experiment has appeared recently
concerning the Rev. John Jones,* of Holywell,
in Flintshire, one of the most prominent
preachers of his day. He was once travelling
alone on horseback from Bala to Machynlleth,
where the country is wild and desolate.
When emerging from a wood he met a
man carrying a sickle. The man had been
seen by the minister at an inn when passing.
In answer to a question, the minister gave
information as to the time by his watch, and a
short time after, noticed the man had furtively
moved into the field, and was running along-
side the hedge, removing the straw from his
sickle as he ran. Then he noticed the man
trying to conceal himself behind the hedge near
the gate through which Mr. Jones would have
to pass. Firmly believing that the man
intended to murder him, the minister bent
his head in prayer. As he did so the horse
became impatient, and started off so suddenly
that the minister had to clutch the reins,
which had fallen on the neck of the steed.
Turning round to see if there was any available

* This is the real name. The story is included by the
kind permission of the Editor of the *Western Mail*.

help, the minister was astonished to find close to his side a horseman in a dark dress, mounted on a white horse. No previous sound had been given of the stranger's presence. Mr. Jones told him of the danger he feared, but no reply was vouchsafed, the stranger simply looking in the direction of the gate. Then the minister saw the reaper sheathing his sickle and hurrying away. The gate was reached, the minister hastened to open it for his mysterious companion, and waited for him. But the guard on the white horse had disappeared as silently and unobserved as he arrived."

And now this chapter will conclude with an account of a very frivolous spirit indeed, for the story of the Riverside ghost must be told. Rarely does one hear of a "spook" with a sense of humour, but that quality, as expressed by a taste for practical joking, was evidently possessed by the intelligence that used to haunt the old house to which we have given the fictitious name of Riverside. Situated in one of the deep and beautiful valleys of South Wales, and belonging originally to the ancient family of Rhys, the house dates back to the time of Henry the Seventh. The last Rhys died about forty years ago, since when the place has changed hands several times, though its present tenants have owned it for a long while, and have apparently been left severely alone by the ghost.

Our story goes back fifty years or more, to a time when a certain Mrs. X. and her infant daughter went to stay at Riverside. One evening after dinner, Mrs. X. went upstairs to see her child (whom she had left sleeping in her own room), but what was her astonishment and subsequent alarm to find the cradle empty. On inquiry and search being made, no trace of the baby could anywhere be found, and the distracted mother rushed off to find her host, and acquaint him with her anxiety. Mr. Rhys received the news with the astonishing remark, " Do not be alarmed ; wait patiently, and the baby will come back." He then went on to say that all in the house were often annoyed by the tricks of the family ghost. Frequently books, garments, umbrellas, anything in fact, if left lying about, would disappear in the most unaccountable way. But if no notice were taken, the articles were always returned in a short time. Mr. Rhys added he was convinced that the ghost had taken the infant, and that she would certainly soon be returned. All this was cold comfort to the poor mother, who found the ghost theory a hard one to believe, and prepared to endure a night of suspense as best she could. Left alone at length by her friend with many exhortations to try and sleep, she could only lie miserably awake, longing for the next day, when search could be renewed. But towards morning, a sudden impulse seized her to get up and look once more at the cradle, when scarcely could she believe her eyes ! For there, sleeping peacefully, lay the missing child, who, it may be added, was never afterwards any the worse for what sounds like a rather unpleasant adventure.

Of the above story I think that " se non è vero, è ben trovato " might well be said! But it is here recounted for what it is worth, as an old tale which probably had more or less foundation in facts of an occult nature.

Another tale of Riverside dealt with a lady in a green silk dress who could be heard rustling about the house, and had also the usual unpleasant ghostly habit of appearing by one's bedside at midnight. But the details— what there were of them—were too vague in character to be worth more than a passing allusion. A pity, as I have always thought there might be interesting possibilities connected with the history of this daintily robed ghost, whose presence in the old house was known by that gentle, feminine sound, the soft rustling of silken attire.

CHAPTER III

" Rest, rest, perturbèd spirit."

MANY stories of haunted houses are told where the disturbing power has seemed to have a distinct object in view, and this object attained, all further manifestations have ceased. Such was the case of a very old farm-house in one of the South Welsh counties. It had long been known that mysterious tappings were constantly heard there, proceeding always from a certain spot in the wall of one particular room. At last this house fell into such bad repair that it had to be partly rebuilt. When the masons were pulling down the wall from whence the tappings came, they found, carefully built into this very wall, an old register-book. It was in a fair state of preservation, and the later entries in it dated from the time of the Commonwealth. They showed that a mason, who could neither read nor write, was then appointed vicar of the parish, and the former incumbent turned out. However, he seems to have remained among his parishioners, performing the offices of the Church in secret, and we may suppose that, taking refuge in the farm-house (which very likely was a place of more importance in those days), the clergyman had the register-book hidden in the wall, to preserve it from falling into the hands of the illiterate mason. The old book has been restored, and is much treasured by its possessor. Since its discovery, the house has been rebuilt, and is now entirely free from the mysterious tappings.

A striking instance of what determination on the part of a ghost can do, comes from Glamorganshire. Mr. Roberts, the owner of a very ancient house in that county, decided for various reasons to let it for a time, and was fortunate in finding a tenant who took it for a term of years, seeming to be delighted with the place. But after he had lived there for a few months, this gentleman wrote to Mr. Roberts saying he could no longer stay in the house. When pressed for reasons, he evaded reply for a while, but at length said "he could not stand the ghost." It appeared that one day, soon after his arrival, he had been sitting quietly reading in one of the rooms, when on raising his eyes from his book, he had been astonished to see "a little old lady" with a "horrible frowning expression" standing close by him. As he gazed at her, she vanished as suddenly and noiselessly as she had come, but this appearance was followed by many others; in fact, the old lady, always with her sinister, frowning look, haunted him. Whenever he least expected her, he was sure to look

round and find her at his elbow. And at last
the apparition had become too much for his
nerves, and he felt he must leave the place.
He added that he was sure the old lady was an
ancestress of Mr. Roberts, who, annoyed at the
family home being occupied by a stranger,
evidently resolved to make herself unpleasant
until she drove him away, in which amiable
resolution she succeeded.

As a rule, new bricks and mortar create an
environment particularly uncongenial to a self-
respecting ghost. Ivied walls, gabled roofs, dim
and musty passages leading to gloomy, oak-
panelled rooms, supply the kind of setting that
the spook of convention demands, and nobody
passing a certain little house close to the road,
just outside the seaside village of Aber——n
would ever think of its being haunted. Built
some fifteen years ago by a retired seaman
named Captain Morgan, this very ordinary
dwelling (of the five-windows-and-door-in-the-
middle style of architecture, absolutely unre-
lieved by gable, porch or balcony) is certainly
far from suggesting any thoughts of the uncanny.
Yet I remember hearing, soon after it was built
and occupied, that it was supposed to harbour a
ghost, though inquiry could elicit little beyond
the fact that Captain Morgan had remarked
to a friend: "I don't know what it is about
my house, but we do hear the queerest noises
that we can't account for. We begin to think
it is haunted." Then people who heard about
these "noises" remembered rather a curious

thing. Soon after the house was begun, while the workmen were engaged on the foundations they came across the skeleton of a man, buried in the earth, and examination revealed that the skull had a hole through the forehead. Instead of keeping these remains together, and having them interred in consecrated ground, the finders carelessly left the bones lying about until they crumbled away and were hopelessly scattered. Whether this discovery had anything to do with the disturbances of which Captain Morgan and his family complained one can but conjecture; time has long since closed the page on which is written the fate which overtook some unknown individual on that spot perhaps a century or more ago, and there is no local tradition to help one to frame a reason for any such deed of violence. However, the inexplicable sounds are no longer heard; and it is said that their cessation dates from the day of a terrible thunder-storm when the house was struck by lightning (though not much damaged), an electric disturbance which seems to have effectually laid, or at least frightened away, the ghost.

Carmarthenshire abounds in tales of ghosts and ghostly happenings. I know one house of great antiquity and historic interest in that county which possesses a spectre of most approved pattern in the person of a headless lady, who, report says, may be met walking along a certain path in the garden by an old yew-tree, at the uncomfortable hour of one in

the morning. She is also supposed to account
for mysterious footsteps sometimes heard in
an upstairs passage. Two people of my acquaintance have heard these footfalls, and
declare they are produced by no human agency.
A family tradition says that dancing must
never take place in the drawing-room; if it
does, the ghost will surely appear among the
company.

But far more interesting than the vague
rumours concerning the "headless lady" (after
all, a most conventional type of ghost) is the
story connected with a maple-tree growing by
the roadside, about a mile and a half from the
house just described. "Once upon a time"
there was a poor tramp, who, walking along
this road (which is the highway to Carmarthen),
sat down to rest at the very place where the
tree now stands. He carried a staff made of
maple-wood, which he plunged into the ground
beside him, and soon, being very tired, he went
to sleep. He never woke again, for while he
slept he was foully murdered. His body, of
course, was found and removed, but nobody
noticed the maple staff, stuck in the ground
beside him; and left there, it took root,
flourished and became the tree one sees there
now. And local belief declares the spot is
haunted. Nothing, say the country people, is
ever *seen;* but after nightfall, no animal, and
especially horses, will willingly pass the tree,
which still marks the scene of an otherwise
long-forgotten tragedy.

If we continued our way along the road for a few miles beyond the maple-tree, we should come to a house said to possess a ghost story, for which, in repeating here, I feel I must apologise, owing to its very apocryphal character. But I cannot resist the temptation to relate it ; as the tale—even if it is untrue, and perhaps it is not—is such an excellent example of the kind that sends one to bed with the "creepy feeling" that all really enjoyable ghost "yarns" should produce. Well, many years ago, a young widow who was related to her hosts, went to pay a visit at this house, and was given a room containing a large, four-post bedstead. The dressing-table was against the wall opposite the bed. One night, as the widow sat before the glass, combing her plentiful locks, and murmuring sadly (we may presume in affectionate remembrance of the departed), "Poor John, poor John," she suddenly saw, reflected in her mirror, a horrid sight. There was the quaint old "four-poster," and, hanging from the top rail, was the body of an old man. History is silent as to the feelings of "poor John's relict" on beholding this terrible reflection, but as she lived in Early Victorian times, it is safe to conclude that she immediately "swooned" and probably had hysterics afterwards. But she subsequently learned that an old miser had once inhabited that room, and had been strangled in that very bed one night for the sake of his money.

It is usually supposed that bodily ills are left behind on our exit from this mortal world, but the tale of a well-known ghost that used to haunt another Carmarthenshire house (now rebuilt) rather contradicts this theory. Owing to the official position of its tenant, a great many people used formerly to be entertained there, and one day a certain guest asked his host which of the servants it was who had such a bad cough. He said that since he arrived, he had constantly heard some one coughing terribly in the passages and on the staircase, but could never see the person, although sometimes the sound seemed quite near him.

The host listened gravely, and then remarked that he was sorry his friend had been disturbed by the cough, which was no earthly sound, but was caused by the " ghost," and had been heard by other people at different times.

The " coughing " ghost had another idiosyncrasy. At this same house a certain bedroom and dressing-room, communicating by a door, were once occupied by a friend of mine and her husband during a couple of days' visit. Now this door between the rooms was carefully shut and latched the last thing at night. In the morning, greatly to my friend's surprise, the door was thrown wide open, although she felt absolutely certain, and so did her husband, that it was firmly shut the night before. It was only a slight incident, but the strangeness of it rather dwelt in Mrs. L——'s mind, until one day after her return home, when

D

she happened to mention it to a neighbour, who remarked : " You must have had the haunted room. It has always been known that the dressing-room door can never be kept shut; no matter how tightly closed the night before, it is always found open in the morning."

For many years local legend has used Brynsawdde, the home of a very ancient Carmarthenshire family, as a setting for various weird happenings. Of these, perhaps the most interesting, and certainly the most inexplicable, is a story that I well remember was current at the time of the late owner's death, who was a well-known character in the country.

It was said that on the day he died a small black dog appeared — from whence no one knew—leapt on the bed, and lay across the dead man's face. Chased away, it disappeared, but was again found sitting on the coffin after the lid had been screwed down. And after the funeral, a whisper went round that " the dog " had jumped into the hearse as the coffin was put in; and that later it had appeared slinking, like some evil thing, through the knot of mourners at the graveside and was never seen again.*

Another story tells how, not many years ago, some people were returning from a dinner-party in the neighbourhood, and as they passed Brynsawdde, which they knew to be entirely

* See remarks in Chapter VI. referring to " Corpse Dogs."

uninhabited, they were astonished to see every window of the house brilliantly illuminated, as if for some great festivity. Nor, on making inquiries, was the slightest explanation of the lights ever forthcoming.

Near the Carmarthenshire border lies the little town of St. Govan's, which, a very few years ago, was much agitated by the pranks of a most inconsequent and noisy ghost. Selecting the abode of one of the quietest and most respected families in the place for the scene of its exploits, it proceeded with demonstrations that not only aroused excitement in the neighbourhood, but for a few days attracted considerable attention from the daily press. But in spite of close investigation no real solution of the mystery was ever arrived at, though the sceptical (and larger) section of the community at length dismissed the matter as a case of trickery in some shape or other, an explanation which, in the light of many reliable witnesses' evidence, was quite inadmissible to thoughtful minds, compelled eventually to relegate the strange happenings to that domain which M. Camille Flammarion has so happily called " L'Inconnu." The first brief report of the occurrences in a local paper ran (slightly altered) as follows : " Great excitement has been caused at St. Govan's during the past week, owing to the alleged appearance in the principal street of a ghost. It has taken up its abode (so the story goes) in the house of Mr. Moore . . .

from which in the early hours of Sunday morning loud metallic clanks were to be heard. Mr. A. B. Rose and others at once proceeded to investigate, and it was found that a bed in one of the rooms was rocking violently, and in doing so, came in contact with the wall, causing the sounds which had been heard. Further investigation failed to reveal the cause of the rocking. The bed was in contact with nothing but the floor, and nothing could be found to indicate in any way that the rocking was caused by anything natural. It is curious that the phenomenon always takes place at about seven in the morning and at the same hour in the evening. . . . This is not the first occasion on which mysterious occurrences have taken place, and many are inclined to attribute them to the supernatural. . . .

" Since Sunday several attempts have been made to solve the mystery, but up to now nothing has been deduced from the observations made. . . . The street opposite the house has been thronged all day, and the aid of the police has had to be called to remove the crowd of sightseers."

The " metallic clanking " referred to above was so loud that it could be heard many yards away from the house, down the street. But though noises and disturbance continued each morning for several days afterwards they were never again as loud and insistent as on that Sunday. Various persons, bent on investigation of a more or less " scientific " order,

soon discovered that by establishing a code of
rappings they could communicate with the disturbing agent, and accordingly each morning,
visitors arriving at the unconventional hour of
6.30 proceeded to the room containing the
mysterious bedstead, and by means of taps
held long conversations with the "ghost."
These taps always came from the same place
on one of the walls. Some curious statements
were thus obtained, and in one case when a
lady (whom I know personally) was the inter-
viewer, some assertions made to her were quite
extraordinary in correctness, containing as they
did information known to no one else in the
town or district. On the other hand, it does
not seem as if anything new or interesting was
imparted to anybody; the answers to questions
in most cases seemed evidently framed to suit
preconceived ideas in the listeners' minds, and
however impressive at the moment, the statements when repeated certainly sounded most
vague and unconvincing, *except* in the one instance referred to. But that the knocks and
rappings were in themselves absolutely genuine,
and produced by some supernormal means, cannot be doubted. Any one who has ever had any
experience of "table-turning" will realise that
this genuineness of manifestation is quite
compatible with the extreme futility of the
"information" usually conveyed in such ways,
and will recognise that the noises and rappings
in the house at St. Govan's evidently belonged
to the same class of phenomena. Manifesta-

tions of such a vehement and insistent order
must surely have had their origin in some
unknown psychic disturbance, some mysterious
jarring sufficient to set quivering the veil between things seen and unseen. And in this
and similar cases it has always seemed to me
that trying, however vainly, to find a reason
for these disturbances is very much more interesting than heeding or dwelling long on
the "messages" which reward the efforts of
the investigator. For if indeed "spirits" are
responsible for the replies to our questions they
seem only too often to belong to that "lying"
class, with whom it is certainly best to avoid
dealings.

In regard to the haunted house of St. Govan's
its history and associations may have had
something to do with the manifestations, for,
as remarked in the previous chapter, there must
be few old houses which have not known strange
happenings within their walls.

This particular habitation, of most unobtru-
sive and unghostlike aspect, is of some antiquity
as houses go in St. Govan's. For many years it
was used as a bank, and long before that, it
was an inn. And surely a "ghost" was ever
a necessary appurtenance to every respectable
inn of the olden days! But no authentic tale
or legend remains to connect those times
with the present, or to furnish a romantic
background for the strange and inexplicable
behaviour of the "St. Govan's Ghost."

And as its noisy demonstrations daily became

less, and at length ceased entirely, so public interest gradually waned; and no definite result having been obtained by any investigator, the subject—after forming for several weeks a sort of conversational bone of contention between sceptics and believers—shared at last the fate of all such abnormal topics, and died a natural death.

High up in one of the wildest and loveliest valleys that pierce the Ellineth mountains, is a house which we will call Nantyrefel. One would like to linger in description of a place possessing a unique charm, which must appeal to all who appreciate the enchantment of beautiful scenery surrounding a house rich in literary and romantic associations. Such a place without a ghost would be incomplete, and accordingly it has the reputation of being most respectably haunted, and by more than one "spook." For reasons of discretion, we cannot here relate the most interesting of the occult incidents connected with Nantyrefel; but to pass its gates without mention of any one of its "revenants" would be impossible, and so the following short tale shall be told.

Rather more than two years ago, a certain lady went to stay at this mountain abode, taking her maid "Brown" with her, a person, one is assured, of average intelligence, and not over-burdened with imagination.

One evening, during the visit, about nine o'clock, Brown had occasion to go up the front staircase, in order to fetch something required by her mistress. Half-way up the stairs she paused, for, descending towards her, came an elderly man, with a long grey beard. Standing respectfully on one side, Brown allowed him to pass, wondering meanwhile who he could be, as she did not remember having seen such a noticeable figure about the house before. Continuing his way down, the old gentleman reached the foot of the staircase, and disappeared round a corner into the hall. He walked very slowly, and the maid, looking round after he passed her, saw, to her great surprise, that his clothes were of the most extraordinary and antiquated cut. Her errand despatched, Brown found her way back to the housekeeper's room, where she remarked to the butler that she had just seen such an odd-looking old gentleman coming downstairs; adding that she supposed he must have arrived by some late train, and was going down to get some dinner. The butler promptly replied that no new visitors at all had arrived at Nantyrefel that day; and when Brown described the long beard and quaint garments of the man she had seen, she was assured that there was no one in the least resembling her description in the house. Yet the maid knew she had not been dreaming, and that she actually had seen the old gentleman, and that moreover he had brushed past her as she waited at the angle of the stairs while he went slowly by.

So it would appear that what Brown really

saw was an apparition, one of those household ghosts with which many an old mansion is peopled, could we but see them; ghosts harmless and timid, with no mission to terrify, or grievances to air, but just indulging a little earthly hankering for an occasional visit to the scenes they loved in life.

Do many people, I wonder, know the strange, uncanny feeling it gives one, to return to a sitting-room at night, after the lights have been out, and the house quiet for an hour or so? One descends to fetch a forgotten book, and pushing open the door, one wishes the candle gave a better light that would reach those far dark corners. For surely the room, so short a time deserted, is nevertheless peopled—and by what? At least, that is the impression I have had, and very odd it is, and one cannot help wondering whether, at the

"very witching time of night,"

the "gentle ghosts" that Shelley writes of, really do creep out of the Invisible, and return for a little space to that human atmosphere, which perhaps some of them may have left many a year ago with regret and sorrow.

And now, from the rather tame incident just repeated, we will turn to a real "thriller" in the way of ghostly experience, namely, the story of Glanwern, in South Wales. Several mysterious tales are told about this house, but the most interesting one (and undoubtedly authentic as far as her own experience goes) was related to me by a Miss Travers, who was asked to stay there a few years ago.

Although there was nothing remarkable about the appearance of the room that was given her, it struck her at once with an odd feeling of nervousness, a feeling that increased so much when she was left alone for the night, that having no night-light, she determined to keep both her candles burning. The hours dragged by, Miss Travers finding sleep out of the question. Suddenly, towards one o'clock, a sound broke the heavy stillness of the night, exactly as if some one had violently pushed open her door and rushed into the room. Imagine her alarm! And the greater, as nothing was to be seen, although the first was followed by a succession of noises resembling the shuffling of feet about the floor, and struggles as of people fighting. After a time the sounds ceased, but poor Miss Travers, too terrified to move, lay quaking, and how she got through the night she never knew, for in an hour or so the same thing occurred again : the door was burst open, and the shufflings and strugglings went on as before. This invisible performance happened *four times* during the night, but on the fourth occasion the struggle seemed to cease very abruptly, and the next sound Miss Travers heard was distinctly that of a heavy body being dragged across the floor towards the door. And as this occurred, she felt a horrible and indescribable sensation of intense cold pass over her like a wave.

Resolved not to spend another night alone, and under the plea of feeling nervous, she asked one of the daughters of the house to sleep in her room for the rest of her stay, but fearing incredulity, said nothing of her experience to her hosts, especially as after the first lonely night there was no repetition of the sounds. But when at a neighbouring house she mentioned where she was staying, her friend remarked, " I wonder if the ghost ever ' walks ' there now." Judicious inquiry from Miss Travers elicited the story that " once upon a time " two brothers lived at Glanwern. One night they quarrelled and fought, one killing the other, and burying the body in a wood near the house. Ever since then the murderer is said to haunt the room where the tragedy occurred.

The following tale, which was related as being absolutely true, I have slightly altered in two or three minor details, to prevent any possible localisation, as it is connected with a very well-known house and family in West Wales. Oaklands will be a good name for the house, and in the sixties and seventies of the last century a certain Colonel Vernon, a widower, lived there as head of the family.

At the time of the story he had invited a young man, named Carter, the son of an old friend, to stay at Oaklands, and besides Carter there was another guest, a Captain Seaton, who was a frequent visitor there, and a contemporary and valued friend of Colonel Vernon.

One night Mr. Carter stayed up reading long after his host and Captain Seaton had gone to bed, and the lights in the house been put out. Indeed, it was nearly one o'clock when he lit his bedroom candle, made his way across the hall, and upstairs on the way to his room. Half-way up the stair made a turn, and it was when he reached this turn and could look back into the hall, which of course was quite dark, that Carter was astonished to see a light coming towards him down a passage which ended near the foot of the staircase. Wondering who could be about so late, and thinking it might be one of the servants, he paused on the stairs, and was somewhat surprised to see the tall figure of a woman emerge from the passage, and begin swiftly mounting the stairs. She wore a kind of loose, flowing garment, and as she passed Carter, who had involuntarily drawn back against the wall, he saw that her face was extraordinarily beautiful. He also noticed the candlestick she carried: it was of brilliantly polished silver, and most curiously shaped in the form of a swan. As the lady (for Carter instantly divined that she was no servant) glided by without taking the slightest notice of him, his astonishment became curiosity, and determining to see what became of her, he followed her up the stairs. Never turning her head, or showing by the slightest sign that she was aware of Carter's presence, she reached the landing, where she stopped a moment, then turned down the corridor where the principal bedrooms were situated. Carter, watching, saw her stop at the third door and enter the room, the door closing softly behind her. Rousing himself from his surprise, Carter proceeded to his own room, but the extraordinary appearance of the lady he had seen, joined to her apparent unconsciousness of his presence, the unusual hour, and the fact that he knew of no woman inmate of the house, other than the servants, produced such bewilderment of mind that he found it impossible to sleep. Early next morning he was astir, and happening to meet Captain Seaton in the garden, he could not forbear relating his nocturnal experience to his fellow-guest.

When Captain Seaton heard the story he looked very grave and asked, " At which door in the corridor did the lady stop ? " Carter replying that it was the third door, Captain Seaton would say no more, remarking that they would discuss the subject again later on, only begging him to say nothing of what he had seen to their host.

Soon after breakfast, Captain Seaton asked Carter to come with him to the pantry, where they found the butler, who had been many years in the Vernons' service. Chatting with the old servant, Captain Seaton presently led the conversation round to the subject of the family plate, remarking how fine it was, and

finally asking the butler to show Mr. Carter
some of the most ancient and interesting pieces
in the collection.   Much of the old silver was
taken out of its wrappings and displayed, and
at length Seaton said, "But where are those
queer candlesticks?   You know the ones I
mean—made in the shape of a swan."   The
butler answered rather reluctantly that the
candlesticks mentioned had been 'put away for
many years, and he feared they must be very
tarnished.   However, on being pressed, he
fetched down from a high shelf in the plate
cupboard, a baize-covered parcel, and from it
drew a silver candlestick, very old and tarnished, but the shape of which, Carter was
startled to see, exactly resembled the one
carried by the lady of his adventure.   Seaton
said to the butler : "You are certain you have
not had these candlesticks out lately?"   "Oh
no, sir," answered the old man, but noticing
Seaton's serious expression, his tone changed
to one of alarm, and he exclaimed, "But what
is   the   matter, sir?   *Has anything been
seen ?*"

Seaton then asked Carter to relate again
what he had seen the night before, and when
he heard that the lady had entered the third
room in the corridor, the butler broke into a
cry of, "Oh, my poor master ! Some grief is
coming to him."

Captain Seaton then explained that the
figure Carter had seen was no human being,
but an apparition, and that her appearance,

carrying the swan-shaped candlestick—always brightly polished—invariably betokened trouble or misfortune for the Oaklands family.

"It was Colonel Vernon's door you saw her open," added Seaton; "let us hope on this occasion her coming has not been for evil," a hope that was unfulfilled, as before the day was over, Colonel Vernon received news that his brother had died the night before.

Most people will agree that there is something particularly unpleasant in the idea of a ghostly animal, though why it should be so is hard to explain. But there is no doubt that the majority of us would prefer encountering a human rather than a four-footed "revenant." The Welsh have a superstition about "hell-hounds," or _cŵn annwn_, as they are called in the Principality. These fearsome creatures are said to hunt the souls of the departed, and generally only their mournful cry can be heard—a sound to make one shudder and tremble. But occasionally a stray hound is seen by some unlucky individual, to whom the sight is sure to bring disaster or death—an old Celtic belief, and most certainly superstition, but it recurs to one's mind in connection with the following story.*

* In his "Welsh Folk-lore" the Rev. Elias Owen says: "The Fairy Dogs howled more at cross-roads and like public places than elsewhere. And woe betide any one who stood in their way, for they bit them and were likely to even drag a man away with them, and their bite was

A few years ago, a certain Mrs. Hudson
went to live near the small town of W——
in South Wales. One day, not long after
her arrival, she and a friend went for a walk
along the high road near the town. On their
way they had to pass a quarry, which was
reached by a gate and path leading off the
road. Just after the two ladies had passed
this gate Mrs. Hudson heard a sound of loud
panting behind her. She stopped, and looking
back, saw a large black dog come running out
of the quarry down the path towards the gate.
Whereupon she said, "I wonder whose dog
that is, and why it was in the quarry."
"What dog?" asked the friend, looking in
the same direction, "I don't see any dog."
"But there is a dog," said Mrs. Hudson
impatiently; "can't you see it standing there
looking at us?"

However, the friend could see nothing, so
Mrs. Hudson somewhat impatiently turned and
walked on, feeling convinced the dog was there,
and marvelling that her friend neither saw it
nor heard its panting breaths.

Soon after this, happening to meet her
brother-in-law, who was an old resident in
the neighbourhood, she asked him who was
the owner of a particularly large black dog,

often fatal. They collected together in huge numbers in
the churchyard when a person whose death they announced
was to be buried, and howling round the place that was to
be his grave disappeared on that very spot; sinking there
with the earth and afterwards they were not to be seen."

describing where she had seen it. The brother-in-law, listening with a rather queer expression, answered, " So you have seen that dog ! Then, according to tradition, either you or your friend will die before six months are past. That was a ghost-dog you saw ; it has appeared to several other people before now, and always forebodes death."

Mrs. Hudson did not pay much attention to what she considered a very superstitious explanation of a trivial occurrence, feeling perfectly certain that what she had seen was a real animal. But it was an explanation she recalled with a feeling of horror, when within six months of the date of that walk, her friend most unexpectedly died. The curious point in this experience is, of course, that the phantom dog was visible to only one of the two friends, and that not the one for whom the warning was intended.

As I have before remarked, there still lingers in some parts of Wales a breath of that atmosphere of fairyland and romance which, to any-body possessing imagination, gives a peculiar value to ideas and beliefs that in less inspiring surroundings would be classed as unmixed super-stition by people of common sense. So that the explanation given to a certain Mr. Blair—who was partly of Highland extraction, and therefore possessed something of the Celtic temperament—of a singular little adventure that befell him in Wales, did not seem to him at all far-fetched at the time, but rather the

one most appropriate, and quite characteristic
of the country. Business obliged Mr. Blair to
live some years in this particular Welsh valley,
and often, after dinner in the summer, he
would cross the river, and walk up the opposite
hill to a house called Wernddhu where some
friends lived, and spend the evening with
them. From Wernddhu a narrow, steep road
led down to the bottom of the hill, where it
ended; and from this point, a grass lane led
up in the direction of a farm.

In the twilight of a certain beautiful evening Mr. Blair left Wernddhu, and started to
walk home. He had his dog, a spaniel, with
him, and as he descended the hill and reached
the place from which the grass lane diverged,
he noticed his dog, who was running in front,
suddenly lie down and begin to whine. And
then he saw that there was another dog, a big
Scotch collie, gambolling and playing round
the spaniel, though where it had come from
he could not imagine, as he was sure that no
strange dog had followed him from Wernddhu.
But as he walked up to the two animals, his
own still whining and shivering, the other
suddenly darted away and disappeared up the
lane that led to the farm, much to the apparent
relief of the spaniel, who immediately seemed
to forget his fright, and became quite lively
again. Blair continued his homeward way,
wondering to whom the collie belonged, as he
did not remember having seen it anywhere
about before. But the incident, slight though

it was, somehow made a decided impression on his mind, so much so, that he could not forbear mentioning it next day to his old landlady, remarking that he supposed they must have got a new dog at Nantgwyn—the farm to which the grass lane referred to eventually led. Mrs. Morgan asked him what the dog was like, and when told, she exclaimed, "Why, indeed, Mr. Blair, you must have seen the Nantgwyn Dog!" She said it was no creature of flesh and blood, but an apparition which had appeared to other people at different times. The story went that many years ago, a tramp had been found lying dead on the very spot where Blair had seen the collie, and it was always thought that the dog, when living, must have belonged to him, and with the devotion characteristic of its kind, had continued faithful, even after death.

Writing of these wraiths of dogs recalls a story told by a Welsh lady whom I will name Miss Johnson, and who was staying during the winter of 1874 with some relations at a house in the West of England. One Sunday evening about six o'clock, when Miss Johnson and the family were sitting quietly in the drawing-room, a great noise was suddenly heard exactly like hounds in full cry. It seemed as if the pack swept past the drawing-room windows, turned the corner of the house, and entered the yard behind. The kennels of the local hunt were only four miles away, and on hunting days the hounds often met or ran in the direction of the house. But to be disturbed by the cry of hounds on a Sunday evening was such an unheard-of thing that Miss Johnson and her friends were, for the moment, petrified with amazement. Almost immediately the butler came running to the room, exclaiming, "The hounds must have got loose! I hear them all in the back yard."

"But how could they get in?" asked some one; "the gates cannot be open at this hour on Sunday." The butler went off looking rather disconcerted, and not a little scared; and Miss Johnson went into the hall, where she found her collie-dog—usually a very quiet, gentle animal—barking and rushing about in a state of frenzy. She opened the front door, and the collie ran out, barking and growling savagely, made a great jump in the air as if springing at somebody or something, then suddenly sank down cowering to the ground, and crept back whimpering to his mistress's side. An exhaustive search revealed not a sign of a hound or stray dog about the place, and Miss Johnson and her relations went to bed that night feeling much puzzled by the strange incident. Next day came the news that a near relative of Miss Johnson had died suddenly the evening before at six o'clock!

Twenty-five years later, Miss Johnson had a similar experience previous to the death of another relation, on which occasion the hour of the death, and the time at which she heard the hounds cry, again tallied exactly. And while meditating on the strangeness of such a coincidence occurring twice over, Miss Johnson remembered the tales that the country people about her old home in Wales used to tell concerning the " Cŵn Teulu " (family hounds) said to haunt the woods round the house, to see or hear one of which was a sure sign of death.

Some people have a vague superstition about the ill-luck of a bird coming into a house, and consider it a sure sign of approaching death should a bird chance to dash itself against a window-pane, as sometimes happens in a gale of wind, or through the attraction of a bright light within the room.

A curious instance regarding this feeling, which occurred quite recently, shows what tremendous power such a superstition may have on certain minds, and how the mind, reacting on the body, may indeed bring fulfilment of what was regarded as a prophecy. The person concerned was a Pembrokeshire farmer, well known to the friend who gave me the story, and whose words I now quote :

" Mr. A. B. Jones, of S——, who was one of the churchwardens of the parish for forty years or thereabouts, died unexpectedly and somewhat suddenly, about three weeks ago. I went the day before yesterday to see Mrs. Jones, who told me all about it, and mentioned the following circumstances. On a cold Sunday evening last winter, just as Mr. R——, the Rector, was going to the pulpit for the sermon, a starling perched on Mr. Jones's head, and remained there : presently he put out his hand, gently grasped the bird, and putting it into his coat pocket, took it home.   He turned it loose in the stable, for he felt sorry for it, and wished to give it a chance of living.   Mrs. Jones said she was, as I know, not superstitious, but was it not odd ?

"It seems that Mr. Jones had had for some months a presentiment that he was not long for this world ; his widow showed me an entry in his diary to this effect, and told me that he had been giving his son, a lad of eighteen, all sorts of instructions not long before his death. Whether he was influenced by the starling incident or not, I cannot say."

(This account was written in September 1907, some months after Mr. Jones's death occurred.)

In a very interesting old work, entitled " Cambrian Superstitions " (published in 1831), the author, William Howells, refers to the Welsh belief in death-warnings brought by birds ; quoting an instance which he mentions as being well known in his day.

" The following remarkable occurrence I cannot refrain from narrating, as the family in which it occurred, who now reside at Carmarthen, were far from being superstitious ; their seeing this will recall it to memory.   As they were seated in the parlour with an invalid lying very ill on the sofa, they were much surprised at the appearance of a bird, similar

in size and colour to a blackbird, which hopped
into the room, went up to the female who was
unwell, and after pecking on the sofa, strutted
out immediately ; what appears very strange,
a day or two after this, the sick person died."

Having previously been told that the invalid
was " very ill," her demise does not appear in
the cold light of print as " strange " as it did
to Mr. Howells, in whose ears the story
doubtless sounded more impressive than it does
when read eighty years afterwards. After
relating another story of the same kind, Mr.
Howells goes on to say, " I have learnt of
several similar instances occurring in England,
and many more are related in Wales; but this
bird has now, I believe, become a ' rara avis in
terris.' "

CHAPTER IV

OTHER GHOSTS

"What beckoning ghost along the moonlight shade,
Invites my steps, and points to yonder glade?"

LET us now stray across the Cambrian border, and pursue some of the "pale ghosts" that one suspects are probably just as numerous in England, Scotland, and Ireland, as in "superstitious" Wales. And looking through my notes, the first story I come across seems quite worthy of repetition, though the incident described was not rounded off by anything sensational in the way of sequel or discovery.

A few summers ago, a certain Mrs. Hunt, who is a relation of some friends of mine, took a house at Blanksea on the south coast for the summer holidays. The house turned out all that was comfortable and convenient, and nothing particular happened while the Hunt family were there. But after they all returned home, Mrs. Hunt noticed that her two boys were continually talking between themselves of somebody called "Bobo." At last one day she asked the children who they meant by "Bobo." They replied, "Oh, she was the little

72

girl who was always about the house at Blanksea, and used to play with us. She didn't seem to have any name, so we called her ' Bobo.' "

Mrs. Hunt was extremely puzzled by this piece of imformation, as she had never seen any strange child in the house, and at length she concluded that it was only some nonsense imagined by the two boys. However, she still could not help thinking a little about the mysterious " Bobo," and eventually determined to make some inquiries about the house ; as to who had lived there, &c. &c. ; and great was her astonishment to learn through these inquiries that the house was always supposed to be haunted " by the ghost of a little girl."

This story reminded me of a very old house near Arundel, in Sussex, said to be haunted by the ghost of a nun ; and it is alleged that the apparition has been seen by children living there. Inexplicable noises are also frequently heard, and a window visible from outside is said to belong to " the nun's room," though the room it really lights is walled up and cannot be entered.

The apparition of a child figures in another very curious tale. I was once told of a certain rectory in one of the English counties, where, during a summer not very long ago, a Mr. Shadwell, by profession an artist, went to stay as a paying guest. He was given a sitting-room of his own, and did not join the family of an evening unless he felt inclined. One evening after dinner he was sitting reading in this room by himself, when the door was quietly opened, and in walked a little girl. The clergyman had several children, with whom Shadwell had already made friends, but this child he had not seen before, so concluded she must have been away from home and had probably only just returned. So he remarked, "Good evening, my dear, I don't think I have seen you before."

However, the child made no reply, and did not even look at him, but walking slowly along the side of the room, she paused, laid her hand on a certain part of the wall, and then turned, and as slowly and deliberately walked out again. Trifling as the action was, there was something so curiously impassive about the demeanour of the little girl, and her absolute indifference to his presence, that it struck Shadwell as extremely odd, and the more he thought of it the more uncomfortable he felt, though for the life of him he could not imagine why. Next morning, when he saw the Rector, he said to him: "I did not know you had another daughter, the little girl who came into my room last evening. Why haven't I heard about her before?" He spoke lightly enough, for a night's sleep had convinced him that life in the country had made him fanciful, and that the impression made upon him by the silent child was due to morbid imagination. So what was his astonishment to see the clergyman appear greatly agitated by his question, and apparently unable to reply at once. Presently he said to Shadwell : "That was no living child that entered your room, but an apparition which has been seen before ; and I beg of you not to mention the matter to my wife, for she always reproaches herself with being partly to blame for the death of that little girl, who was our eldest-born." He then told the artist that a few years previously they had had workmen in the house, doing some plastering and papering. One day, while the work was going on, the Rector's wife had wished to pay somebody some money, and remembering that she had just left half a crown on her dressing-table, she told her eldest girl to run upstairs and bring down this coin. But after rather a long interval, the child returned saying the money was not there. Whereupon the mother became annoyed, knowing she had really left the half-crown on the table, and told the child she must have either stolen the coin or else be playing a trick for mischief. The little girl obstinately denied all knowledge of the money, so she was sent to bed in disgrace, where she presently fell into such a terrible fit of sobbing and crying that an attack of convulsions came on, and finally she became unconscious and died. To the parents' grief was added remorse, caused by the torturing doubt that the poor child might have been after all unjustly blamed for a fault committed perhaps by one of the strange workmen, for the missing half-crown was never found.

Shadwell listened thoughtfully to this sad story, and later, after thinking over the incident of the evening before, in connection with the tragic circumstances of the child's death, an idea struck him. He at once sought the Rector, and asked him whether he had ever thought of having the wall examined at the spot to which the apparition had pointed. On hearing that this had not been done, he asked permission to investigate, and, with the clergyman's help, he opened the wall. And there, embedded an inch or two in the plaster, exactly where the child's hand had been placed the night before, was a half-crown!

Now was this merely a wonderful coincidence? Or may we believe that the little girl, having hidden the coin in the tempting surface of the wet plaster—whether for mischief or her own gain one cannot tell—was afraid to confess her fault? And Death overtaking her, could not give the spirit rest, till its efforts to reveal the truth had been recognised and understood.

But it is certain that since the discovery of the coin in the wall the apparition of the child has never again been seen.

Another rectory that possessed the reputation of being haunted is that of Clifton, in Kent. This is a very old house, dating from the fourteenth century, and, according to my informant, who knew the house well (a relation of his having held the living from 1869 to 1880), mysterious noises had often been heard there by different individuals. One lady who was paying a visit reported having a "dreadful night," "with people walking up and down the passage, and muffled voices," but no one had left their rooms all night. And a youth of sixteen or seventeen, employed as an outside servant, declared that once when an errand brought him into the house, he saw "an old gentleman in a grey dressing-gown walk down the stairs before him, and suddenly disappear." Whatever it was he saw, the boy was so thoroughly frightened that he would never enter the house again. My friend's letter continued: "Mrs. Lowther (whose husband, the late Dr. Lowther, succeeded my relative as Rector) when 'moving in' elected to stay the night in the rectory by herself, instead of returning to . . . London. The workpeople left, and a village woman, having prepared Mrs. Lowther's evening meal and made up fires for her in sitting-room and bedroom, went home. *Something* is said to have occurred during the night, and Mrs. Lowther acknowledged (so the writer has been told) as much, but would never say what it was that had alarmed her; but it is believed that she *did* say that nothing would induce her again to be alone in the house at night."

I once went to tea with the wife of Canon C——, in the cathedral city of E——. In the course of conversation the subject of "ghosts" came up, apropos of which Mrs. C—— remarked : "As you know, these houses are exceedingly old, being actually part of the ancient Norman monastery adapted to modern use. Very odd and unaccountable noises were for a long while heard in the house next door to ours, which of course is all part of the same old building; and these noises were vaguely ascribed to 'the ghost,' though nothing was ever seen. But, at last, some structural alteration of the house became necessary, and in the course of this work the discovery was made of a human skeleton, which had evidently lain hidden for centuries, and presumably was that of a Benedictine monk. The bones were carefully buried, and from that time no more noises have been heard."

This story rather resembles the tale of a much more interesting ghost which inhabited an old manor-house in Somersetshire, and which succeeded for many years in keeping human beings out of the place. Time after time the house would be let, people always making light of its haunted reputation, or else determining to brave its terrors. But they never stayed more than a few weeks, when they invariably went away, declaring that one or more members of the household had seen an apparition on the main staircase. The description—and rather horrible it was— was always the same. The figure of a woman would come gliding downstairs, carrying her head under her arm, and on arriving at the foot of the stairs she invariably vanished.

At last there came a tenant bolder than his predecessors, and gifted with an inquiring turn of mind. He said he liked the place and meant to stay there, and if possible evict the ghost. And he at once began to investigate. Beginning at the attics he tapped and sounded every wall and suspicious-looking board in the house, with no result in the way of discovery till he reached the principal staircase. This, being the ghost's favourite haunt, received special attention, and working his way patiently down step by step, he found at length under the old flooring at the foot of the stairs, a hollow place of considerable size. And in this hole reposed, *headless*, a human skeleton (which subsequent examination proved to be that of a woman) with *the severed skull lying by its side.* Then the enterprising tenant hied him to the Vicar of the parish and told him of the grisly find, and after due consultation it was decided to collect the poor remains and bury them decently in the churchyard, a ceremony which seems to have effectually "laid" the ghost, as report says it has never since been seen.

But to return for a while to the city of E——. The best ghost story I heard there concerns the Bishop's Palace, a beautiful Tudor house, said to be built on the site of the great monastery for which E—— was famous in

Saxon times, and the predecessor of the Norman building, of which parts still survive in the modern canons' residences.

I was told that at some time during the sixties or seventies of the past century, a certain friend of the reigning Bishop was invited to stay a night at the Palace. He had never been at E—— before, and therefore knew but little of its history or traditions. There was nothing at all extraordinary in the appearance of the room assigned to him, and he slept well enough for the first few hours after going to bed. But towards morning he woke, and though he knew himself to be wide awake and not dreaming, yet he had a terrible vision. He was first roused by sounds which appeared like people scuffling and struggling, and almost immediately he seemed to be aware in some way of a dreadful scene being enacted in his room. Although all was dark, yet he saw, as if by some extra sense, that a man dressed in what looked like very ancient armour was lying on the floor, while another figure in a monk's habit, knelt on, and was apparently trying to kill him. The vision—or whatever it was—lasted but a few moments, then the whole picture faded, and all became still again. The rest of the night passed undisturbed, though further sleep was impossible for the visitor, so great was the sense of horror and absolute reality left in his mind by the scene he had witnessed, and the sinister sounds he had heard. In the morning he sought the

Bishop, to whom he described his experience, and who listened gravely; answering that his friend's story was very remarkable in the light of an old tradition connected with the house, and with the Saxon monastery which it was believed anciently occupied the site of the Palace. At the time of the Norman invasion, the community numbered only forty monks; who, feeling themselves a small and undefended company, and probably fearing local disturbances and possible pillage, when the Conqueror's coming should be known, hastened to apply to William for protection. In reply the grim Norman sent forty of his knights to be billeted on the monastery, saying that each monk should have a knight to defend him. Such a claim on their hospitality was probably rather more than the holy men had bargained for, but the arrangement seems to have worked well enough, until at last a sad tragedy occurred. One of the monks having quarrelled (we are not told why) with his foreign guardian, and quite oblivious of the danger he was thereby bringing on his companions, rose up in the night and murdered the warrior, taken unawares in the darkness. What followed history does not relate, but no doubt William was careful to exact suitable vengeance for his slain follower.

There is a curious mediæval painting still to be seen in the Palace, representing the forty Saxon monks and their knightly protectors.

Still one more story of a haunted rectory

F

must be told, a story which when I heard it made a considerable impression on my mind, from the fact that it was related by a person who, I feel sure, would stoutly deny that she " believed in ghosts." And so her incredulity regarding matters pertaining to the world beyond our five senses made her recital all the more convincing.

Several years ago this lady, Miss Robinson, chanced to spend a summer with the rest of her family at a certain country rectory, which her father had rented for a few months. It should be stated that the neighbourhood was new to the Robinsons ; none of them had ever been in the county before, and when they first went to the rectory they did not know any of the residents around.

It happened one evening when the days were very long, and there was still plenty of light left, that Miss Robinson was going upstairs about nine o'clock followed by her little dog, which half-way up passed her and ran on to the stair-head. There it suddenly stopped short, looking down a passage which led off the landing, and exhibiting every symptom of fear, shivering and whining, and its hair bristling. Miss Robinson thought this behaviour on the animal's part rather odd, but as she gained the landing and looked down the passage, wondering what had frightened her dog, she distinctly saw a man cross the end of it and apparently disappear into the wall. As there was no door at the spot

where the figure vanished, Miss Robinson
thought this still more curious, but as she
saw nothing further, and the dog also seemed
immediately reassured, she began to think
they had both been victims of a hallucination,
and resolved to keep the matter entirely to
herself.

A short time afterwards she went to tea
with some neighbours who had called on them ;
and after the usual conventional inquiries as
to how they liked the place, and so forth,
Miss Robinson and her sister were asked, "if
anything had been seen by them of the rectory
ghost ? " Instantly Miss Robinson's thoughts
flew back to that evening on the staircase,
and her dog's terror. However, in reply, she
only asked what form the "ghost" was supposed to take. The answer was that a former
inhabitant of the house had murdered his wife,
and that ever since, the murderer's ghost was
said *to haunt the end of the passage* which
led off the landing. As she listened to these
words, Miss Robinson could not repress a little
shudder at the remembrance of the mysterious
figure seen by herself and her dog at the very
spot described. But no repetition of her experience ever occurred, nor was the apparition
seen by any one else in the house during the
time the family stayed there.*

* Mr. Leadbeater would probably class this " ghost " as a
" thought-form."   " Apparitions at the spot where some
crime was committed are usually thought-forms projected
by the criminal, who, whether living or dead, but most

There is a curious story told of a country house of some antiquity in North Devon. This house was once let to a Mr. Barlow, who took up his abode there, and presently asked a friend to stay with him. This friend's name was Sharpe, and he was put into a room containing an old and handsome four-post bed. Next morning, Barlow asked Sharpe what sort of a night he had had. "Very bad," was the unexpected reply. "I could not sleep for the talking and whispering going on—I suppose—in the next room. I hope you will ask the servants not to make so much noise to-night." Barlow accordingly spoke to the servants, who promptly denied having been anywhere near the guest's bedroom, or having sat up late at all. But the following day Sharpe had again the same complaint to make; he could get no sleep on account of the tiresome "whispering" going on round him all night. Much mystified Barlow suggested a change of apartment to his visitor, who refused, saying he would rather wait another night and try to find out the cause of the disturbance. Barlow then said he would sit up with Sharpe; and accordingly the two retired to the room at bed-time, and putting out the light, awaited

especially when dead, is perpetually thinking over and over again the circumstances of his action. Since these thoughts are naturally specially vivid in his mind on the anniversary of the original crime, it is often only on that occasion that the artificial elementals which he creates are strong enough to materialise themselves to ordinary sight."—"The Astral Plane."

developments. Presently, sure enough, a whisper was heard, and very soon the room seemed full of whispering people. After listening amazed for some time, Barlow struck a match, when immediately the sounds ceased, nor, although both men carefully examined walls, chimneys, windows, and every nook and corner anywhere near the room, could they find a sign of a human being, or any possible reason for the extraordinary manifestation. But both noticed with astonishment that, whereas the curtains had been pulled back off the bed, ready for occupation, they were now pulled *forward*, and the ends neatly folded up on the pillows as a bed is left in the day-time.

After this Sharpe changed his room for the rest of his stay, but Barlow made diligent inquiries until he found out all that he could about the previous history of the house, and particularly of the room containing the four-poster. He learnt eventually that the big bed had been for many generations in the house, and had always been used when there was a death in the family for the lying-in-state of the corpse.

Another Devonshire house, D——n Hall, the ancestral home of an old and well-known family, is haunted by a lady who sometimes surprises visitors unaccustomed to her little ways.

On one occasion a husband and wife, who happened to be staying at D——n, were both dressing for dinner on the first evening of their visit. Suddenly, without any warning, the door of the wife's room was opened, and in walked a beautifully dressed woman, with grey or powdered hair turned off her forehead and worn very high. Without appearing to take the slightest notice of Mrs. Blank the intruder passed through the room, opened the dressing-room door, went in and shut the door behind her. Petrified with astonishment, Mrs. Blank stood for a moment staring after the apparition, then dashing into the dressing-room she exclaimed, "Where did that lady go?" (There was no other door except the one communicating with the bedroom.) The husband, who was calmly dressing, was naturally somewhat surprised at the question; explanations followed; he had seen nothing and thought his wife must have been dreaming. But overflowing with wonder, Mrs. Blank went downstairs, and seeking her hostess confided to her the singular incident, adding that she supposed the "lady" was a fellow-guest who had in some way mistaken her room; but where had she disappeared to when she entered the dressing-room? "Hush," was the reply. "It was no living person you saw, but the *ghost*; only don't breathe a word to any one else here. There is no harm in her; and she has often been seen before by people staying in the house." And with this casual explanation Mrs. Blank was fain to be content.

A story very similar to the above is told by

Mr. Henderson in " Folk-lore of the Northern
Counties " about a house in Perthshire, where
the figure of a very beautiful woman was one
evening seen on the staircase by a visitor
staying in the house. In this case the hostess
informed her friend that the apparition had
frequently been seen before, but always by
strangers, never by any member of the family.

The following incident is said to have happened quite lately in another Scotch country
house. Two sisters, one quite a young girl,
went to stay at this place, and were given
rooms close to one another. One night the
younger sister suddenly woke up. The room
was dimly lighted by a bright moon, and there,
close by the bed, the girl saw, apparently rising
out of the floor, a human hand. Thinking she
had nightmare she closed her eyes and vainly
tried to sleep, but feeling impelled, in spite of
fear, to look again, there was the hand—
nothing else—close by her bedside still. This
time she felt horribly frightened, and hurling
herself out of bed, she rushed to her sister's
room, which she insisted on sharing for the
rest of the night. In the morning she told the
elder girl what she had seen, declaring she
could not pass another night in that room.
Her sister scolded her a little for what she
considered foolish imagination, and begged her
to say nothing of the " bad dream " to their
friends, as people did not like it to be thought
that there was anything ghostly about their
houses.

Later in the day the son of the family was taking the elder sister over the house, which was old and interesting. Presently he remarked, "We have a ghost here, too, you know." The visitor pricked up her ears, and asked what form the ghost was supposed to take. "It is a hand," was the reply, "nothing else." "Then my sister saw it last night," exclaimed the girl, whereupon she was much surprised to see her companion turn pale and seem agitated. But in reply to her questions he would say nothing further, leaving his listener wondering uncomfortably if the appearance of the spectral hand was a bad omen; and if so, whether it boded ill to the owners of the house or to the individual who had had the disagreeable experience of seeing it.

Before leaving Scotland we must mention an Aberdeenshire house, described to us by a friend as inhabited by the ghost of an old lady, who regularly appears in a certain room once a year. Evidently her unrest is caused by an uneasy conscience, if tradition be correct; which says that she was a wicked old person who flourished in the early seventeenth century. Having a deadly feud with a neighbouring family, she decoyed them with false promises and an invitation to a feast into the tower of the house. Then she had the doors locked, and setting fire to the tower, she got rid of her enemies in one horrible holocaust.

From Scotland to Northumberland is not a

far cry, and on our way South you must listen
to an odd little story connected with a house
called Wickstead Priory in that county. The
friend who told me was staying at Wickstead
when the incident happened. I will call her
X.; and her room happened to be on the
opposite side of the corridor to a large bedroom
occupied by a married sister of the hostess.
One evening, while X. was dressing for dinner
she heard some noise and commotion going on
in this other room, and later in the evening,
she asked its occupant what had been the
matter. "Oh," was the reply, "I had such a
fright!" I am sure you won't believe me, but
as I sat doing my hair before the looking-glass,
a *horrid-looking little monk* came and peered
over my shoulder. I saw him plainly in the
glass, but when I turned round, no one was
there!"

I have before remarked on the disagreeable
habit so common amongst ghosts of appearing
by one's bedside at dead of night. In fact,
a large percentage of the ghost stories one
hears contain the words, "He (or she) looked
round, and there was a figure standing by the
bed," &c. &c. And a tale which I heard on
excellent authority of a Staffordshire house
concerns a "bedside" spook of the most
conventional pattern, which succeeded in
thoroughly astonishing, if not alarming, a
Colonel and Mrs. West, who were paying a
visit to Morton Hall. The owner of the house
was a cousin of Colonel West's, whom he had

not seen for a long time, and of whom he knew little, having been soldiering abroad for many years. On the first night of their visit, towards the small hours, Mrs. West woke up quite suddenly, and although the room was dark, yet she could somehow perceive distinctly a figure advancing towards the end of the bed, seeming to emerge from the opposite wall. Very startled, Mrs. West woke her husband, who also saw the figure—by this time stationary at the foot of the bed—and called out to it, "Who are you, and what do you want?" But at the sound of the voice the figure retreated, and seemed to fade away. The rest of the night passed undisturbed.

Next morning Colonel West said to one of the children of the house, "A nice trick you played us last night." For after much discussion, he and his wife had come to the conclusion that the only reasonable explanation of what they had seen was that they had been the victims of a clever practical joke. The child addressed looked puzzled, and when questioned said that nobody had played any tricks at all. Later on, their hostess came to Mrs. West, and said she was extremely sorry to hear from her little girl that they had been disturbed the night before, adding that owing to the house being full the Wests had been given the *haunted room*. For knowing they were complete strangers to Morton, and probably knew little of its traditions, it was thought very unlikely they would be troubled by anything uncanny. They were then asked what they had seen, and Mrs. West described the mysterious "figure," saying that it resembled a woman wrapped in flowing garments, and carrying a bundle under her arm. "That was the ghost," replied the cousin's wife. "Years ago a woman was murdered in that room, and ever since then she has occasionally appeared to people, dressed as you describe and carrying her head under her arm."

Wherein lies the decided element of creepiness contained in my next story? Perhaps it may be that it deals with a haunting of a most unusual and remote character, having its origin in some unknown disturbance of the very elements themselves. It relates to a very well-known English house called Ainsley Abbey, where not so very long ago there was a large party staying for the local hunt ball; among the guests a certain Mrs. Devereux. Knowing that she would be very late returning from the ball, this lady told her maid not to wait up for her, but to go to bed at her usual time. So what was Mrs. Devereux's surprise when she came back in the early hours of next morning, to find that the maid had disobeyed her injunctions, and was waiting in her room. When asked why she had not gone to bed, she told her mistress that she had done so but had been so disturbed by the "terrible storm"—thunder and great gale—that she could not rest and grew too frightened to stay in her room. She sought the house-servants, but to her surprise they had noticed no storm, and laughed at her when she said there was a high wind raging round the house. Finally she resolved to wait in her mistress's room, adding that she was thankful the party had got back safely, as she had felt concerned at Mrs. Devereux being out in such awful weather. As the night had been perfectly calm and fine, Mrs. Devereux was much astonished at this tale, but at last concluded (though she did not say so) that her maid must really have been asleep and dreamed of the storm. But happening to mention the matter as a joke to her host next day, she was surprised to find it treated with the greatest interest, and to be told it was no case of a dream. That occasionally people who came to stay at Ainsley *could* hear sounds that they always described as a thunder-storm and hurricane of wind blowing round the house. In fact, it was a species of haunting which had never been accounted for. Like an echo of Dante's

> " Infernal hurricane that never rests,
> Hurtles the spirits onward in its rapine;
> Whirling them round."

Not long ago, I came across a lady who told me of some very interesting happenings of a ghostly nature connected with a house in a suburb of one of the great University towns. This house was taken by a Mrs. Drew, in order that she might be near her son, who was an undergraduate of one of the colleges. But he lived with his mother, who also took in three other undergraduates as paying guests. After a time Mrs. Drew discovered that there was something rather unusual about this house. She heard noises she could not account for, and frequently had the consciousness of an invisible presence in the room with her. But at last one day, she not only *felt* but *saw* quite near her, an appearance, as of the head and shoulders of a very pretty, amiable-looking girl, the head draped in a kind of veil. After this, she would sometimes become aware that the same apparition was sitting beside her ; on other occasions she would see it dimly flitting about the rooms ; but in time she got so accustomed to its appearance that she took little notice of it at all.

Once, when her son went up to the North to play in a cricket match, Mrs. Drew felt rather worried about him, as he had not been well, and she was afraid he was not really fit to play. Especially during the night after the match, she could not help lying awake and thinking about him. Suddenly she became conscious that the now familiar figure of the apparition was standing at the foot of the bed, looking at her. And then, for the first time, it spoke to Mrs. Drew, telling her to feel no alarm for her son's welfare, " for," it said, " I have been with him all day. He is quite well, and played very well in the match." Then it disappeared.

On another occasion, young Drew and one of

his friends were reading at night in the study, when they were startled by the sound of a terrific crash in the next room. They rushed in, expecting they knew not what, but the room was empty, quiet and dark.

One summer Mrs. Drew tried to let the house for a while. A lady came to see and appeared on the point of taking it ; but while discussing the subject with Mrs. Drew in the drawing-room, and making final arrangements, she quite suddenly got up and went away, saying she would write. When her letter came, it merely said the house did not suit her ; but later, when pressed for an explanation of such a sudden change of mind, she admitted that while talking to Mrs. Drew in the drawing-room she had observed a beautiful young girl come and seat herself on the sofa close by them. No one else seemed to see the girl or to be in the least conscious of her presence ; yet somehow her appearance produced such an uncanny feeling in the visitor's mind that she felt she could not stay another moment in the room or in the house. And so she broke off the negotiation.

At last, her son's time at the University being finished, Mrs. Drew gave up the house, and was succeeded in it by some people who opened a shop. And while making the alterations necessary for the purpose, the work-people discovered hidden under a floor the skeleton of a young woman ! But who she was, and why her bones were there, no one

had been able to find out at the time when I
heard the story—about two years ago—though
imagination promptly offers us a choice of
sinister theories to account for the buried
skeleton and its restless *umbra*. "Requiescat
in pace" for the future!

Why the foregoing tale should remind me of
a ghost that was seen in a Northamptonshire
house, I do not know; but, in spite of the
irrelevance, here is the story. Some years ago,
a large party was assembled there for shooting,
and one of the guests was given a rather out-
of-the-way room, which was usually allotted to
a stray bachelor, when, as happened on this
occasion, the house was very full. However, it
was a very comfortable room, and the visitor
slept there soundly enough on the first night,
until at what seemed to be a very early hour,
a knock on his door woke him up. Mechani-
cally saying "Come in," he opened his eyes,
and saw a little elderly man, dressed in rather
tight-fitting, pepper-and-salt clothes, such as
grooms wear, who walked into the room with
an assured step, pulled up the blind, and went
out again. Mr. Blank imagined that the man
had come to call him, though wondering why
he came so early and had brought no hot
water; especially as a footman called him later
at the usual hour. When asked next morning
if he had slept well, he mentioned the fact
of his being awakened so early, saying he
supposed that the man must have made some
mistake. "What was he like?" asked the

host, and when his friend described the man as elderly, and looking like a groom, his friend replied, "What you say is rather odd, because only a fortnight ago, a groom, who was an old family servant here, died. Of late years he had done little work, but almost until the end, one of his duties, which he would never relinquish, was *to call any one who chanced to occupy that room.*"

My next tale has always seemed to me one of the most interesting psychic experiences that I have ever heard related.

Some few years ago, a young officer, whom we will call Lestrange, went to stay at a country house in the Midlands. It may be said that he was a good type of the average British subaltern, whose tastes, far from inclining towards abstract study or metaphysical speculation, lay chiefly in the direction of polo, hunting, and sport generally. In fact, the last person in the world one would have said likely to "see a ghost." One afternoon during his visit, Lestrange borrowed a dog-cart from his friend, and set out to drive to the neighbouring town. About half-way there he saw walking along the road in front of him a very poor and ragged-looking man, who, as he passed him, looked so ill and miserable that Lestrange, being a kind-hearted person, took pity on him and, pulling up, called out, "Look here, if you are going to C——, get up behind me and I will give you a lift." The man said nothing but proceeded to climb up on the cart, and

as he did so, Lestrange noticed that he wore
a rather peculiar handkerchief round his neck,
of bright red, spotted with green. He took
his seat and Lestrange drove on and reaching
C—— stopped at the door of the principal
hotel. When the ostler came forward to take
the horse, Lestrange, without looking round,
said to him : " Just give that man on the back
seat a good hot meal and I'll pay. He looks
as if he wanted it, poor chap." The ostler
looked puzzled and said : " Yes, sir ; but what
man do you mean ? "

Lestrange turned his head and saw that the
back seat was empty, which rather astonished
him and he exclaimed : " Well ! I hope he
didn't fall off. But I never heard him get
down. At all events, if he turns up here, feed
him. He is a ragged, miserable-looking fellow,
and you will know him by the handkerchief
he had round his neck, bright red and green."
As these last words were uttered a waiter who
had been standing in the doorway and heard
the conversation came forward and said to
Lestrange, " Would you mind stepping inside
for a moment, sir ? "

Lestrange followed him, noticing that he
looked very grave, and the waiter stopped
at a closed door, behind the bar, saying : " I
heard you describe that tramp you met, sir,
and I want you to see what is in here." He
then led the way into a small bedroom, and
there, lying on the bed, was the corpse of a man,
ragged and poor, *wearing round his neck a red*

G

handkerchief spotted with green. Lestrange made a startled exclamation. "Why, that is the very man I took up on the road just now. How did he get here?"

He was then told that the body he saw had been found by the roadside at four o'clock the preceding afternoon, and that it had been taken to the hotel to await the inquest. Comparisons showed that Lestrange had picked up his tramp at the spot where the body had been discovered on the previous day; and the hour, four o'clock, was also found to tally exactly.

Now was this, as the ancients would have told us, the *umbra* of the poor tramp, loth to quit entirely a world of which it knew at least the worst ills, to "fly to others that it knew not of"? Or was it rather what Mr. C. W. Leadbeater has described in his book, "The Other Side of Death," as a *thought-form*, caused by the thoughts of the dead man returning with horror to the scene of his lonely and miserable end, and thereby producing psychic vibrations strong enough to construct an actual representation of his physical body, visible to any "sensitive" who happened that way? We must leave our readers to decide for themselves what theory will best fit as an explanation of this strange and true story.

And now for the curious experiences of a professor of a well-known theological institution, which he related most unwillingly and under great pressure to a small gathering of friends, amongst whom a friend of mine was present, who afterwards, knowing my interest in ghostly lore, told me the stories.

This professor, whom we will call Mr. Bliss, was a graduate of one of the newer Universities. Some years after he had taken his degree, he had occasion to return to his University, and resolved to put up at his former lodgings, as he would have to make some little stay. So leaving his luggage at the station, he walked to the house, but before going in, he took a turn or two up and down the pavement to finish a cigarette he was smoking. While he was doing this, he saw a man, whom he recognised at once as the son of the landlady, run up the steps and enter the house, shutting the door behind him. His cigarette finished, Bliss followed the man, and knocking at the door was warmly welcomed by his old landlady, who told him she would certainly take him in, adding, " You can have my son's room." " But your son is at home," said Bliss. " Oh no, he is abroad," was the reply, and as Mrs. X. spoke, Bliss saw a shadow come over her expression. " But that is impossible. I have just seen your son go into this house," and he told the mother how he had been smoking, and had seen the man whom he recognised as her son enter the house a few moments before himself. Nor could Mrs. X.'s continued assertions, that her son, far from being in the house was not even in England, shake the conviction of Bliss that he had seen the man in question only a few minutes before. However, seeing that the subject was distressing to Mrs. X. he said no more. When night came, the landlady told him that she had decided to give him her own room, taking herself the one formerly used by her son. Bliss went to bed, and at first slept well, but very early next morning he was roused by a sound as of some one creeping softly into the room. He struck a light, and to his intense surprise saw Mrs. X.'s son walking stealthily across the room to a corner where there stood an old closed bureau. The man apparently took not the smallest notice of Bliss, who, watching him, saw him take a key from his pocket, and unlocking the bureau, fumble in its recesses until he drew out what appeared to be a bag of money. This was too much for Bliss, who, convinced that he was witnessing an act of robbery, whether by young X. or somebody cleverly impersonating him he had no time to consider, jumped out of bed and rushed at the intruder, on whose shoulder he brought his arm down with some violence. But imagine the horror of Bliss, when instead of being checked by a human body, the blow encountered—nothing ! And even as he stood there, the apparition—for such it surely was— vanished utterly.

Next day Bliss felt impelled to tell Mrs. X. of his astonishing experience, and (passing over the painful excitement and emotion aroused by his recital) he heard the following story, which seemed to afford a possible if somewhat far-

fetched explanation of an extraordinary happening. It appeared that young X. was far
from being an exemplary character, and that
he ended his various escapades by robbing his
mother. He had entered her room in the night
and by means of a false key opened her bureau,
where he knew she kept money, and removed
all that was there. After which he had left the
country, and was living abroad, never, of course,
having been home since.

So much for one experience; the other is
more dramatic, and happened on the same
occasion of Bliss's visit to his old University.
One afternoon, he went for a long walk into
the country, and it was quite dark when he
returned homewards. As he proceeded along
a deep lane, so overhung with trees that the
gloom on either hand seemed almost impenetrable, he became aware of a dim light
approaching him, and presently he saw that it
came from the head of a figure who was
walking towards him and who, as it drew nearer,
seemed to be dressed like a Sister of Mercy, in
a blue dress and large white cap, while always
the strange, pale light seemed to radiate from her
head. She walked straight and swiftly towards
him, and Bliss saw that unless he moved they
would collide; so, thinking that the person
did not see him in spite of the light she carried
about her, he quickly stepped aside to let her
pass. As he did so, he stumbled over what
seemed to be a large bundle on the road, and,
stooping down to see what it was, he discovered

that the bundle was really a man, lying
huddled up and inanimate, but whether drunk
or otherwise unconscious it was impossible for
the moment to tell, for utter darkness had again
fallen, the woman with the light having absolutely disappeared. But Bliss could now hear
the sound of wheels and a horse being driven
very fast; indeed, had he not loudly shouted,
he and the unconscious man must have been
run over. And what about this man, if he had
not happened to find him lying there? And
again, how *would* he have found him if the
figure with the light had not come by, and
caused Bliss to step aside. Such thoughts
came to his mind, as he helped the driver to
lift the man into the trap, and gave directions
for him to be taken to the nearest hospital;
while further reflection during his walk home
convinced him that any ordinary explanation
of such an incident was quite inadequate, and
that perhaps it was just one of those " things "
that, as Hamlet reminded his friend, are
undreamed of " in our philosophy."

This chapter shall conclude with a tale told
me lately by a friend who had herself heard it
on excellent authority. It concerns a Mrs.
Borrow who, two years ago, happened to be
staying at Fontainebleau. One evening she
thought she would go for a walk, and accordingly setting out, soon found herself free of the
town, and in a deep country lane. Suddenly,
at some distance ahead of her, but still quite
near enough to see plainly, she saw the oddest

figure of a man jump down from the hedge into the road. He wore a curious kind of cap, red, with a tassel hanging down, and his costume altogether appeared more like a fancy dress than the garb of the present day. He stood in the middle of the road, and then Mrs. Borrow noticed that a deer, which had wandered from the forest into the lane, evidently saw the man too, for it stood quite still, gazing fixedly at him. Mrs. Borrow hurried on, wishing to get a closer look at such a strange person, but to her great bewilderment, as she drew near he seemed to vanish away, causing her to wonder if she and the deer had both been the victims of an optical delusion. At all events, she saw no more of the mysterious figure that evening, though, as may be imagined, her mind was full of the occurrence, and as soon as she returned to Fontainebleau she sought out some friends who were residents there, and described what she had seen. They instantly exclaimed : " Oh, you have seen 'le Grand Veneur.' How unlucky for you. He always presages misfortune to those who meet him in the forest." They then explained that " le Grand Veneur " was really a ghost, and told Mrs. Borrow the legend relating to him.

It must be added that so far, happily, the omen has not worked in Mrs. Borrow's case, as no particular misfortune had befallen her when my friend heard the story, only a few months ago. So perhaps the powers of " le Grand Veneur " for " ill-wishing " those who see him have lapsed with time.

Mr. Henderson mentions this apparition in "Folk-lore of the Northern Counties": "Near Fontainebleau, Hugh Capet is believed to ride. . . ." And again: "I have said that the Wild Huntsman rides in the woods of Fontainebleau. He is known to have blown his horn loudly and rushed over the palace with all his hounds, before the assassination of Henry the Fourth." Henderson, it will be noted, describes the huntsman as mounted, while Mrs. Borrow's apparition was on foot; as, however, her description seems to have been immediately recognised as "le Grand Veneur," a well-known ghost, it is probable that Henderson refers to the same tradition.

In a note to his version of the German ballad of "The Chase," Sir Walter Scott relates the legend of the "Wild Jäger," or Wild Huntsman of Germany, adding: "The French had a similar tradition concerning an aerial hunter who infested the forest of Fontainebleau." Also in "Quentin Durward" he mentions "le Grand Veneur," to meet whom in the forest was a bad omen; and again in "Woodstock" he writes of a similar apparition, said to haunt the woods of Woodstock: "Anon it is a solitary huntsman, who asks you if you can tell him which way the chase has gone. He is always dressed in green, but the fashion of his clothes is some five hundred years old."

In a former chapter I have mentioned the alleged appearances in quite modern times of two phantom hunters in Wales. The fact seems to be that the " Wild Huntsman " legend is one of great antiquity and wide distribution, its details in different places being merely altered to suit local circumstances.

But that is a fact that does not in the least detract from the interest of Mrs. Borrow's strange little adventure in the lane near Fontainebleau.

CHAPTER V

CORPSE-CANDLES AND THE TOILI

" A vague presentiment of his pending doom
Like ghostly footsteps in a vacant room
Haunted him day and night."

WHEN St. David of blessed memory lay dying his soul was greatly troubled by the thought of his people, who would soon be bereft of his pious care and exhortations. He remembered the Celtic character, apt to be lifted to heights of enthusiastic piety by any passing influence of oratory, and, alas! prone to sink to depths of indifference, or even scepticism, when that influence was removed. So the Saint prayed very earnestly for his flock that some special sign of divine assistance might be granted them. Tradition says that his prayer was heard, and a promise given that henceforth no one in the good Archbishop's diocese should die without receiving previous intimation of his end, and so might be prepared. The warning was to be a light proceeding from the person's dwelling to the place where he should be buried, following exactly the road which the funeral would afterwards take. This light, visible a few days before death, is the *canwyll corph* (corpse-candle).

Such is the legend generally supposed to be the foundation of a very ancient belief, though a less common version is given by Howells in his "Cambrian Superstitions" (1831), where he says: "The reason of their (the candles) appearing is generally attributed to a Bishop of St. David's, a martyr, who in olden days, while burning, prayed that they might be seen in Wales (some say in his diocese only) before a person's death, that they might testify that he had died a martyr. . . ." The Bishop alluded to here was Ferrars, who was burnt at Carmarthen under the persecutions in Queen Mary's reign.

But whatever the origin of the *canwyll* belief, it was once almost universal in some parts of Wales, and even in these sceptical days one sometimes comes across it in out-of-the-way corners of the Principality.

In Brand's "Antiquities" we read : "Corpse Candles, says Grose, are very common appearances in the counties of Cardigan, Carmarthen, and Pembroke, and also in some other parts of Wales; they are called candles from their resemblance, not to the body of a candle, but the fire, because that fire, says the honest Welshman, Mr. Davies, in a letter to Mr. Baxter, doth as much resemble material candle-light as eggs do eggs; saving that in their journey these candles are sometimes visible and sometimes disappear, especially if any one comes near them or in the way to meet them. On these occasions they vanish, but presently reappear behind the observer and *hold their Corpse* (*sic*). If a little candle is seen, of a pale bluish colour, then follows the Corpse of some Infant, if a larger one, then the Corpse of some one come to age. . . . If two Candles come from different places and meet, two Corpses will do the same, and if any of these Candles be seen to turn aside through some bypath leading to the church the following Corpses will be found to take exactly the same way. Sometimes these Candles point out the place where people will sicken and die. . . ."

The " honest Welshman " above quoted by Grose was the Rev. J. Davies of Geneurglyn, and the whole of his letter, which Richard Baxter published in his " World of Spirits " (1656), is most interesting to read. He continues : " Now let us fall to evidence. Being about the age of fifteen, dwelling at Llanylar, late at night, some neighbours saw one of these candles hovering up and down along the river-bank, until they were weary of beholding it ; at last they left it so, and went to bed. A few weeks after came a proper damsel from Montgomeryshire to see her friends, who dwelt on the other side of the river Istwith, and thought to ford the river at that very place where the light was seen, being dissuaded by some lookers-on (some, it is most likely, of those who saw the light) to adventure on the water, which was high

by reason of a flood; she walked up and
down the river-bank, even where, and ever
as the aforesaid candle did, waiting for the
falling of the water, which at last she took,
but too soon for her, for she was drowned
therein. . . . Some thirty or forty years since,
my wife's sister being nurse to Baronet Rudd's
three eldest children, and (the Lady mistress
being dead) the Lady-comptroller of the house
going late into the chamber where the maid-
servants lay, saw no less than five of these
lights together.   It happened a while after
this, that the chamber being newly plastered
and a grate of coal-fire therein kindled to
hasten the drying of the plaster, that five
of the maid-servants went to bed as they
were wont, but as it fell out, too soon, for
in the morning they were all dead, being
suffocated in their sleep by the steam of the
newly tempered lime and coal.   This was at
Llangathen in Carmarthenshire."

I have always been much interested in this
story, as the house where the accident
happened two hundred and fifty years ago is
very well known to me in these days.   And
indeed the tradition of the five smothered
maids is still extant; for the tale, substantially
as related by Mr. Davies, was told me only a
few years ago by an old woman living in
Llangathen village, who had been many years
in service in the house referred to by Baxter's
reverend correspondent, though the Rudd
family has long disappeared, and the place

changed owners many times since. As to
"Llanylar" on the river "Istwith" it is a
village not so far from my own home in
Cardiganshire; and quite lately a clergyman,
born and brought up in that district, informed
me that when he was a boy—and he is not
old—stories of "corpse-candles" abounded
there, and belief in them was very common.

To return to "Cambrian Superstitions"
again, its author relates what he seems to
think a well-authenticated instance of a
canwyll's appearance, as follows. "Some years
ago (he was writing in 1831), when the coach
which runs from Llandilo to Carmarthen was
passing by Golden Grove (the property of
the noble Earl Cawdor), three corpse-candles
were observed on the surface of the water,
gliding down the stream which runs near the
road; all the passengers beheld them, and it
is related that a few days after, some men
were crossing the river near there in a coracle,
but one of them expressed his fear at venturing,
as the river was flooded, and remained behind;
the other three possessing less discernment,
ventured, and when about the middle of the
river, lamentable to relate, their frail convey-
ance sank through the weight that was in it,
and they were drowned."

Writing in 1888 of Pembrokeshire, Mr.
Edward Laws, in "Little England beyond
Wales," says: "It would be by no means
difficult to find a score of persons who are
fully persuaded that they themselves have

been favoured with a vision of the mysterious lights," adding, "St. Daniel's cemetery, Pembroke, is a likely place for ' fetch-candles.' "

Although the weird privilege was supposed to belong entirely to St. David's diocese, yet some writers mention the belief as well known in North Wales. George Borrow, in " Wild Wales," describes in Chapter XI. a conversation he had on the subject with a woman who lived near Llangollen, and had herself seen a *canwyll corph*. And in our days, Sir John Rees writes in " Celtic Folk-lore " : " It is hard to guess why it was assumed that the *canwyll corph* was unknown in other parts of Wales. . . . I have myself heard of them being seen in Anglesey." But earlier authors nearly always assign South Wales as the real home of the tradition. Meyrick, in his " History of Cardiganshire " (1810), speaks of St. David obtaining the privilege for his diocese, adding : " The *canwyll corph* is bright or pale according to the age of the person, and if the candle is seen to turn out of the path that leads to the church, the corpse will do so likewise."

Scientifically approached, the corpse-candle is merely the well-known *ignis fatuus* (will-o'-the-wisp or marsh light) occasionally seen to quiver and flicker at night over the surface of bog and swamp. Shelley writes :

> " As a fen-fire's beam
> On a sluggish stream
> Gleams dimly."

Often appearing in the distance like a carried lantern, these lights have been known to lure unwary travellers from a safe path to insecurity and danger. Scott's name for the will-o'-the-wisp is Friar Rush's lantern :

> " Better we had through mire and bush
> Been lantern-led by Friar Rush."

In the same connection, Milton in " L'Allegro " also mentions the " friar's lantern."

But though one may have an open mind on the subject of the *canwyll corph*, yet it does not seem as if the *ignis fatuus* explanation covers quite all the ground suggested in the various instances of the *canwyll's* appearance described in the following notes.

All authorities agree that the most characteristic feature of the corpse-candle's appearance is, that it invariably follows the exact line that will be taken by the funeral procession. This is well illustrated by an instance that occurred some years ago at a house in Cardiganshire. Instead of going straight along the drive, the light was seen to flicker down some steps and round the garden pond; and when the death occurred the drive was partly broken up under repair, and the coffin had to be taken the way indicated by the corpse-candle. At another place in the same county, tradition says that before a death takes place there, a corpse-light is always seen to emerge from the neighbouring churchyard, and pass quivering up the drive towards the house. Another

story from Carmarthenshire relates how shortly
before a death in the family owning a certain
house, the woman living at the lodge saw a
pale light come down the drive one evening.
It pursued its way as far as the lodge, where
it hovered a few moments, then through the
gates, and out on the road, where it stopped
again for several minutes under some trees.   On
the day of the funeral the hearse, for an unexpected reason, was pulled up for some time
at the exact spot where the *canwyll* had
halted.

The following story, which was related by a
lady of cultured mind and much common sense,
has always seemed to me one of the most
interesting of its kind that I have ever heard.
Whether it was a case of *canwyll corph* or not
must be left to my readers to determine, but it
is certainly hard to account for the incident in
any ordinary way :

My friend, Miss Morris, lived when she was
a young girl in Wales, and her father's house
stood on a steep hill-side, with the village church
just below, a short walk from the lodge gates.
One Sunday evening, in winter, Miss Morris,
her sister, and two maids walked down to the
church to attend the six o'clock service.   As
they came out from the drive on to the road,
they saw flickering down the hill in front of
them, a pale bluish light, which, in the darkness, Miss Morris and her sister took to be a
lantern carried by some church-goer like themselves, although they could see no figure of

H

man or woman. The light stopped at the churchyard gate, and turned in, but Miss Morris observed that the person carrying it did not enter the church, but went on towards a grave with a tombstone. Now this grave happened to be the only one in the burying-ground, for the church had only lately been built, and the churchyard but newly consecrated. Arrived at the solitary tombstone, the light suddenly disappeared. The two girls went round to the same place, as their curiosity was roused by the light's disappearance, but there was nobody by the grave. Rather puzzled, they went into the church, where they had to wait some time for the service to begin, as the Vicar was very late. Afterwards he told Miss Morris that he had been detained at a cottage by a dying woman, who had begged him to stay with her till the end. When they returned home, the sisters told their mother of the light they had seen, and were promptly advised by her to speak to no one else on the subject, and to dismiss it from their minds as soon as possible. However, next day, as Miss Morris was passing the churchyard gate, she saw a brother of the deceased woman standing there with the Vicar, to whom he said: "My sister wished to be buried by the side of her friend, Sarah Jones." And the man then walked through the churchyard, *straight to the exact place by the tombstone* where Miss Morris and her sister had seen the light disappear on the evening before.

Not long ago I was talking about the *canwyll corph* and kindred subjects with the postmistress of a Cardiganshire village, who remarked that she had only known one person who had ever seen a "corpse-light." This was a woman—now dead—called Mary Jones, and to use the words of the postmistress "a very religious and respectable person." At one time in her life she lived in a village called Pennant (its real name), a place well known to me, where the church is rather a landmark, being set on top of a hill. Mary Jones invariably and solemnly declared that whenever a death occurred among her neighbours, she would always previously see a corpse-candle wend its way up the hill from the village to the churchyard. And at the same place she once saw the Toili (a phantom funeral). This last experience was in broad daylight, and was shared with several other people who were haymaking at the time, and who all saw clearly the spectral procession appear along a road and mysteriously vanish when it reached a certain point. But we will speak of the Toili presently.

Another belief relating to the *canwyll* was that it not only boded future troubles, but that it was positively dangerous for anybody who saw one to get in its way. I had never heard locally of this disagreeable attribute of the corpse-light until I talked to the postmistress already quoted. This woman said that long ago she and other children were

always frightened from straying far from home
by tales of "Jacky Lantern," a mysterious
light, which, encountered on the road, would
infallibly burn them up! George Borrow
("Wild Wales," Chapter LXXXVIII.)mentions
meeting with the same belief when talking to
a shepherd who acted as his guide from the
Devil's Bridge over Plinlimmon. Borrow said:
"They (corpse-candles) foreshadow deaths,
don't they?" To which the shepherd replied:
"They do, sir; but that's not all the harm
they do. They are very dangerous for anybody
to meet with. If they come bump up against
you when you are walking carelessly, its
generally all over with you in this world."
Then followed the story of how a man, well
known to the shepherd, had actually met
his death in that weird manner. Howells
also mentions the same idea in "Cambrian
Superstitions," where, writing of corpse-lights,
he says: "When any one observes their approach, if they do not move aside they will be
struck down by their force, as I was informed
by a person living, whose father coming
in contact with one was thrown off his
horse."

This certainly adds to the fear inspired by
the sight of the *canwyll*, but the more general
belief seems to have been that these lights
were quite harmless in themselves, and when
seen were regarded with awe only as sure
harbingers of future woe.

If we may believe the Rev. Mr. Davies,

whose letter, published in Baxter's "World of Spirits," has been already quoted, there is yet another kind of fire apparition peculiar to Wales, called the Tanwe, or Tanwed. " This appeareth to our seeming, in the lower region of the air, straight and long . . . but far more slowly than falling stars. It lighteneth all the air and ground where it passeth, lasteth three or four miles or more for ought is known, and when it falls to the ground it sparkleth and lighteth all about. These commonly announce the death . . . of freeholders, by falling on their lands, and you shall scarcely bury any such with us,. be he but a lord of a house and garden, but you shall find some one at his burial that hath seen this fire fall on some part of his lands." Sometimes these appearances have been seen by the persons whose deaths they foretold, two instances of which Mr. Davies records as having happened in his own family.

When reading the above description of the " Tanwe "—of which I had previously never heard—there came to my mind a story told me by an old Welsh lady of an extraordinary phenomenon, which she solemnly declared had preceded the death of her brother-in-law— a gentleman well known and respected in Cardiganshire. Shortly before his last and fatal illness his wife, returning home one evening, was amazed to see the most curious lights, apparently falling from the sky immediately over their house. From the account given

by my friend, her sister seems to have at
once recognised the supernatural character
and sinister import of the mysterious lights;
their appearance being recalled with melancholy interest by her and her sisters after
the sad event which so soon followed. Can
this incident be explained as a survival of
the old " Tanwe " idea, of which our authority,
the then Vicar of Geneurglyn, wrote in the
seventeenth century ? It seems as if it might
be so, and that belief in the Tanwe was
probably an old *local* superstition, peculiar
to that district; considering the fact that the
parish of which Mr. Davies was Vicar is in the
same county and not more than a dozen miles
from the house where the fiery death-signals
are supposed to have been seen twelve or
fifteen years ago. For so far I have neither
heard nor read of the Tanwe ⸀being known in
any other part of Wales.

Belief in the Toili used to be very widely
spread in Cardiganshire, especially, it is said,
in the northern part of the county. Meyrick,
the historian of Cardiganshire, tells us : " The
Toili . . . is a phantasmagoric representation
of a funeral, and the peasants affirm that when
they meet with this, unless they move out of
the road, they must inevitably be knocked
down by the pressure of the crowd. They
add that they know the persons whose spirits
they behold, and hear them distinctly singing
hymns." But the Toili was not always visible;
sometimes the presence of the ghostly *cortège*

would be known merely by the sudden feeling
of encountering a crowd of people and hearing
a dim wailing like the sound of a distant funeral
dirge.

Those of us who have lived in the country,
and know how characteristic of a Welsh burial
is this singing of funeral hymns—one or two
of which are of a poignant sadness impossible
to describe—can imagine how significant and
suggestive such a ghostly sound would be to
peasant ears. An old woman, whom I knew
well years ago, used always to declare that
she heard this hymn singing before the death
of any friend or neighbour. She would invariably say, if one commented on any death
that occurred: "Yes, indeed, but I knew
some one was going; I heard the Toili last
week."

I have heard of two cases of people being
involved in invisible funeral processions, which
must truly be a most disagreeable experience.
One story relates to a Mrs. D——, who lived
in the parish of Llandewi Brefi, in Cardiganshire. Her husband was ill, and one day as
she was going upstairs to his room, she had
a feeling as of being in a vision, though she
could *see* nothing. But the staircase seemed
suddenly crowded with people, and by their
shuffling, irregular footsteps, low exclamations,
and heavy breathings she knew they were
carrying a heavy burden downstairs. So
realistic was the impression, that when she
had struggled to the top of the stairs she

felt actually faint and weak from the pressure of the crowd. A few days later her husband died, and on the day of the funeral, when the house was full of people, and the coffin carried with difficulty down the narrow stairs, she realised that her curious experience had been a warning of sorrow to come.

The other instance was told me by the Rev. G. Eyre Evans of Aberystwith (who kindly allows his real name to be given), a minister and writer on archæological subjects of considerable local fame. In his own words :

" As to the Toili, well, if ever a man met one and got mixed in it, I certainly did when crossing Trychrug * one night. I seemed to feel the brush of people, to buffet against them, and to be in the way ; perhaps the feeling lasted a couple of minutes. It was an eerie, weird feeling, quite inexplicable to me, but there was the experience, say what you will."

Quite lately a friend writes from South Cardiganshire telling me of "a ghostly hearse and followers, seen recently by a neighbour, the man recognising the driver of the hearse and the chief mourner . . . and little thinking it was a ghostly procession he was looking at, he whipped up his horse to get closer. . . . The animal reared and trembled, refusing to go nearer or move even in the direction taken by the hearse. Terror then also seized the man, and he turned and fled the longest

* A high hill in Cardiganshire.

way home to avoid the ghostly burial-ground."

Another story of the Toili comes from St. David's, and this we will also give in the words of the correspondent who, knowing my weakness for "ghosteses," was kind enough to send it.

"An old lady, one Miss Black, who is still living, resided some time ago in the house formerly belonging to the Archdeacon of St. David's, with one servant-maid, whom on a certain evening she sent on an errand, telling her to return at once. This she did not do, and in consequence was found fault with. The girl stated, in explanation, that she had been greatly frightened by coming across a phantom funeral descending the steps below the entrance gateway towers (of the Cathedral) and that it turned to the right in the direction of the Lady Chapel. The old lady was incredulous, and said, moreover, that funerals never entered the Cathedral yard (this was, of course, before the yard was closed for burials) that way, which was the fact; they used to pass down the road running parallel with the yard, and enter by the big gate below the Deanery.

"But actually not long after a real funeral did come by the way the girl said, and went in the direction she described; the road referred to being for the time impassable, having been dug across for the laying of some pipes."

The next very good example of this strange second sight also comes from St. David's, and it is through the courtesy of the Editor of the *Western Mail* that I am able to relate it here: "The following anecdote was related by the late Mr. Pavin Phillips, the Haverfordwest antiquary, of a friend of his, a clergyman resident at St. David's. One of his parishioners was notorious as a seer of phantom funerals. When the clergyman used to go out to his Sunday duties, the old woman would frequently accost him with, 'Ay, ay, Mr. —— *fach,** you'll be here of a weekday soon, for I saw a funeral last night.'

"On one occasion he asked her, 'Well, Molly, have you seen a funeral lately?' 'Ay, ay, Mr. —— *fach,*' was the reply; 'I saw one a night or two ago, and I saw you as plainly as I see you now, but you did what I never saw you do before.' 'What was that?' 'Why,' replied the old woman, 'as you came out of the church to meet the funeral, you stooped down and appeared to pick something off the ground.' 'Well,' thought the clergyman to himself, 'I'll try, Molly, if I can't make a liar of you for once.' Some time afterwards the good man was summoned to a funeral on horseback. Dismounting he donned his surplice, and moved forward to meet the procession. The surplice became entangled in his spur, and as he stooped to disengage it he suddenly thought of the old woman and her vision. Molly was right, after all."

Our next story, recounting a most curious

* *Fach*, a mild term of endearment in Welsh.

incident which happened a comparatively short time ago in my own neighbourhood, certainly sounds incredible. Yet I have reason to believe in the truthfulness of the clergyman whose experience is narrated, and should judge him incapable of even wishing to invent any such extraordinary adventure as befell him one night only a few years ago.

Mr. Harris is the Vicar of Llangaredig (which I substitute for the real name), a pretty country church with a comfortable vicarage just across the road from the churchyard. At the time of our story the Vicar's pony was sick, and feeling very anxious about the animal, he determined to sit up one night, in order to see how it got on. About midnight he thought he would go out and have a look at the pony, which was in a stable · exactly opposite the churchyard, with the road between. As the Vicar emerged from the stable into the road he was surprised to hear the sound as of many footsteps, while he immediately had a queer feeling of people pressing round him. In a minute or two he heard wheels as of traps and carriages driving up to the churchyard gate and stopping there, and especially the sound of a heavy vehicle like a hearse. Then, after a pause, came the unmistakable, hollow sound of the hearse door, as it was slammed to on an empty interior.

Then followed the heavy tread of men, bearing a burden into the church. But all this time Mr. Harris *saw* nothing. Rooted to the spot with amazement, he waited a while at the stable-door till the night's stillness was again broken by the sound of many people coming out of church.   Past him they brushed invisibly, then came the roll and rattle of wheels, as traps and gigs drove away.   Then as the crowd seemed slowly to move off, the Vicar *distinctly heard talking*, and though he could not distinguish the words spoken, yet he plainly recognised the voices of two or three of his parishioners.   When all at last was still, Mr. Harris returned to the house, much mystified by his inexplicable experience, which he was presently forced to regard as a prophecy.   For next day came a telegram, informing him that a relation *of the people whose voices he had recognised* had died, and requesting him to arrange for the burial of the deceased in Llangaredig churchyard.

Much resembling these accounts of the Toili in Wales is the experience of certain persons possessing second sight, of whom Martin writes, in his "Description of the Western Islands of Scotland": "Some find themselves as it were in a crowd of people, having a Corpse which they carry along with them, and after such Visions the Seers come in sweating and describe the People that appeared ; if there be any of their Acquaintances among them, they give an account of their Names, also of the Bearers, but they know nothing concerning the Corpse."

So that in ancient times belief in the Toili

may have been common to several of the Celtic tribes, and its origin is possibly of great antiquity. Corpse-candles, too, seem to have been known in Scotland, judging by Scott's allusion, in his ballad of " Glenfinlas "—

" I see the death-damps chill thy brow,
   I hear thy warning spirit cry;
The corpse-lights dance—they're gone, and now . . .
   No more is given to gifted eye."

—though the "lights" here mentioned more probably refer to the vivid blue flames which seers declared to be visible hovering over a dying person. Such a "superstition" is possibly supposed to be extinct; yet this phenomenon has been witnessed by a friend of mine (need I say of Celtic race?) who described the tiny flames as "dancing," using exactly the same word as Sir Walter Scott does.* It seemed impossible to disbelieve my friend's statement, which was made with the utmost solemnity and carried conviction at the moment; yet what can we think as to the absolute truth of it and the many alleged appearances of the Canwyll Corph and the Toili? It is difficult indeed to say. No doubt large "grains of salt" must be taken with some of the stories, while on the other hand one cannot entirely

* In " Folk-lore of the Northern Counties " Mr. Henderson says : " They believe in the county of Sussex that the death of a sick person is shown by the prognostic of 'shell-fire.' This is a sort of lambent flame, which seems to rise from the bodies of those who are ill and envelop the bed."

discredit the testimony of sane and sober
individuals, such as Mr. Harris, or Mary
Jones, the " very respectable and religious "
friend of the postmistress. Personally I have
no wish to be too sceptical; partly on the prin-
ciple that all these ancient beliefs and legends
help to add interest and lend a glamour to a
world ever becoming more matter-of-fact and
material. And also to quote the words of the
great French scientist, M. Camille Flammarion,
because " Ce que nous pouvons penser . . .
c'est que tout en faisant la part des superstitions, des erreurs, des illusions, des farces,
des malices, des mensonges, des fourberies, il
reste des faits psychiques véritables, digne de
l'attention des chercheurs."

CHAPTER VI

CORPSE-CANDLES AND THE TOILI * (*continued*)

"O that's a meteor sent us, a message dumb, portentous,
An undeciphered solemn signal of help or hurt."

THE stories and experiences contained in this chapter consist of material relating to the "Canwyll Corph," the "Toili," and other beliefs, which were collected by the late Lledrod Davies, an inhabitant of the village of Swyddffynon, near Ystrad Meurig, in Cardiganshire.

He was a young man of delicate constitution, but gifted with that intelligence and zest for knowledge which distinguish so many of our Welsh people, and which, when joined to ambition and steadiness of character, are apt to carry them far in worldly progress. And this love of knowledge, and a native shrewdness untrammelled by any smattering of modern education, combined to form many a delightful character amongst our old-fashioned peasants, a few of whom still survive, though the type is fast dying out. If we may believe the descrip-

---

* I am indebted to Mr. Owen M. Edwards, the Editor of *Cymru*, for his kind permission to publish the translations included in this and Chapter VII.

tions in "Wild Wales," George Borrow met many such people in his travels through the Principality, but that was nearly sixty years ago, before the flower of our rural population had begun to migrate to "the Works"—as they call the mines and iron foundries of Glamorganshire.

However, we are digressing from Lledrod Davies, who it seems had intended to enter the Church, but died before he could be ordained. Apparently he was always much interested in the legendary lore and superstitions of his native county, and for a long time had made a point of collecting all the curious tales and experiences he could glean on these subjects; and as the district to which he belonged happens to be remarkable for all kinds of uncanny occurrences in the way of "corpse-candles," fairy legends and the like, he had no doubt a wide field for research. His object in collecting all this information seems to have been exactly the same as my own in a similar pursuit; namely, that he thought it too quaint and interesting to be allowed to die with the old generation, to whom a firm belief in these occult happenings was a matter of course. Also, in the spirit of the true folklorist, he had intended if he had lived to endeavour to trace a connection between these old Welsh beliefs and the folk-legends of other countries. But he died before he could accomplish this object, and after his death (which took place in 1890, at the age of thirty-three) his MSS. relating to these subjects were collected by friends, and published locally in a little pamphlet entitled " Ystraeon y Gwyll "—in English, " Stories of the Dark." This pamphlet, now out of print, was lent to me a short time ago, and partly because its contents concerned my own county and several districts that I know, it interested me so much that I asked and obtained permission to translate and republish the tales contained therein. As folk-lore these are really valuable, for they were noted down exactly as Mr. Davies heard them from the lips of the country people, free from all self-consciousness, and with no idea that they were relating anything but what were fairly common experiences amongst themselves and their friends.

In my translation I have occasionally made use of abbreviation, and I have sometimes slightly paraphrased the original text, here and there rather weighted by repetition, a trait which, however quaint and characteristic in the vernacular, is apt to sound tedious in our more precise and reserved English language. But with these small limitations, I have kept as nearly as possible to Mr. Davies' narrative, which, he tells us, he wrote down as well as he could in the words used by his informants. I will pass over his general description of " corpse-candles," because most of it would only be a recapitulation of what I have already told in the last chapter. But he mentions an interesting item connected with the superstition of which I had never heard before ; to the

I

effect that people who saw the candles were able to judge how soon the death which they prognosticated would occur. If the light were seen in the evening, death would follow quickly; if in the depths of night, the fatal event would be delayed a while. And it is said that there was scarcely ever a mistake made in this calculation of time.

I will now proceed in Mr. Davies' words, heading each incident with the title given it in the collection, and the first is called

THE OLD WOMAN WHO SAW HER OWN CORPSE-LIGHT

In the quiet village of S—— there dwelt an old woman, poor, of miserable appearance and very ragged in clothing.

The only light that entered her cottage came through the door; in a word, the whole business of the house took place at the door. Even the smoke generally escaped by it, although it is true there was a chimney. In such a place had the old woman chosen to pass the rest of her life. She spent many of the long summer days on her door-step, knitting in hand, exchanging the gossip of the season with her friends; while in winter she would be found sitting by the hearth, near a wretched heap of ashes or a bit of turf fire.

One very cold winter evening, as she sat in her accustomed place, knitting her stocking, and humming an old hymn-tune or ballad, she saw something like a spark fall from her bosom into the ashes of the fire before her, where it glittered very brightly. Thinking to find out what the spark was, she seized the tongs, and searched about with them in the ashes. She drew the tongs backwards and forwards through the ashes, and while so doing, she perceived the spark jump up again from the hearth, and go out through the door, and she herself got up and went to the door to see what direction it took. She looked out, and there before her was the little spark become a great light; so bright that it lit the whole place. She took courage to look well at it, she said, in order to make sure what it was. She saw it go out of the house rather slowly, onward along the road towards the burial-ground, to which it was probable that in the course of nature she would ere long be carried. Then, overcome by fear, she went back into the house, and afterwards fell very ill, because she felt quite sure that it was her own corpse-light she had seen, and no other. She related what had happened to her friends, and in truth it was not long before her body followed its light to the burial-ground, there to be re-united. This old woman was noted for seeing and hearing spirits, corpse-candles, and the Toili. Whenever she said to her friends, "There will soon be a burial at such and such a house," they were quite certain the prediction would come to pass.

The next story tells of possible danger connected with seeing a corpse-light.

THE OLD WOMAN WHO WAS BLINDED FOR A MONTH BY A CORPSE-LIGHT

This time it was one of the most wonderful things I have heard in connection with a corpse-light. An old woman, considered one of the best nurses in the country, was made blind by the light. She was always remarkably fortunate in her cases, and chiefly for the reason that she was a seventh daughter. Because it is considered very lucky to have as your doctor or nurse a seventh son or daughter. So because she was lucky, she was universally in request by all the good-wives far and near.

On a certain night the farmer's wife at G—— was taken ill, and Elli the nurse must be sent for, and they despatched the servant-man at once to fetch her. She lived not far from G——, but the road was very rough. The servant mounted a horse and away he rode with much diligence. And very quickly he reached the nurse's dwelling. He told his errand, and it was not long before both set out on the way back. It was a beautiful starlight night, but there was no moon at that season.

The old woman went on horseback, and the servant behind her. They were going along as fast as they could, when the woman asked the man, " Dost thou see a light, Tom ? "

"I don't see one ; where do you see it ? "

"I tell thee it is coming along the road, down from Bont Bren Garreg."

" Oh, I see it now," said Tom.

The old woman knew it at once for a corpse-light. They went on talking about the light, and Tom said in his opinion it was perhaps the light from that house or the other. Now there was a cross-road * on the road along which the light was coming. On they went until they came to the main road, in which place there was a turn, and as they approached the turn, Tom the servant said, " Well, if there was no light before, good-wife, here is one now." And there it was in their midst, on the road and bushes, every corner of the compass was illuminated. They had now stopped at the house. The old woman went in and fell fainting, and when she came to herself, she was quite blind, and could see nothing. They put her to bed and when the morrow brought daylight, she went home. And a month passed before she saw again as usual. After the old nurse went home the servant had to go out again to fetch the mistress's mother. Now he was obliged to go along the road where the light had been, and

* In Welsh folk-lore cross-roads always figure as likely spots for uncanny happenings.

past the churchyard. Away he went and very quickly came in sight of the burial-ground, where, to his fright and agitation, he saw the light again ! For as he came opposite the graveyard, he plainly saw the light inside, and carefully noticed the exact spot at which it lingered.

The old woman declared that some one would most surely soon be brought along that road to be buried, which came to pass very quickly after the light's appearance, this showing that it was indeed a corpse-candle. She also told Tom where the grave of this person would be in the churchyard, which he remembered, and found to be at the exact spot she described. Although this old woman in her day had seen scores of corpse-candles after nightfall, yet this was the most wonderful she ever saw, because of its direct connection with what followed. For its effect could be seen, and Tom the servant, who was an eye-witness of it all, bore testimony of the circumstances from the beginning to the end.

The two following incidents show how the identity of the doomed individual was known.

HOW TO KNOW WHOSE LIGHT IT WAS

In old times I have heard numbers of elderly people assert that they could tell one whose was the " light " passing by, and could relate how this was possible; and with my own ears I have heard one man say how his fear of the thing decreased as he came to know its mystery. One way was to mind and be near running water, or any pond that happened to be conveniently near the road along which the light was coming.

As soon as the light was to be seen approaching, one should stop near the water or the running brook that the candle had to cross, and therein would be seen a reflection of the person whose light it was. Apparently the illumination of the light showed it in the water. There was always a mysterious light on the breast of the doomed individual. One man told me how he had seen the corpse-light after hearing a sound like a great report, whereupon running to some water he found out the person who was to be buried. Though he had seen other corpse-lights from time to time, yet he had never happened to be near water until a certain night. He had been very late, he said, at the smithy, having a ploughshare sharpened, and had a middling long way to return home from the forge. As he was going along the road, he saw a light in the far distance, coming towards him. He did not suspect any harm at the moment, and hastened along, keeping his eye on the light, until he got to the bottom of a slope, up which he had to go. He had a big old cape over him, and for convenience, he folded the skirts of it round his middle. As he straightened himself after doing this, he perceived the light just at his side, and realising that it was a corpse-candle, he determined to see whether the saying was false or true that one could see whose light it was. Now there happened to be a little brook crossing the road at that place. As the light went by he looked carefully into the water, and saw therein a woman he knew very well. He went home much frightened. A little time after, that woman was stricken with illness, and when she subsequently died it happened that her body was carried along that very road for burial. Afterwards he saw a man's light, and that time again it was near water. He resolved to try and know whose it was. He saw the light reflected in the water, and knew the person at once as the gamekeeper in that neighbourhood. Though the keeper was in good health at the time, yet very soon afterwards he fell ill and died, and his funeral too followed the course the " candle " had taken.

THE SMITH OF LLANFIHANGEL AND
THE CORPSE-LIGHT

There was yet another way of knowing whose corpse-candle was seen. This way of finding out required more nerve than the other, for the reason that one must go to the churchyard, through the graves, and inside the church door, and there wait until the corpse-candle came in. And there, as if he were going in his body to church, would be seen the doomed person. This required great determination and bravery as may easily be seen, and for this reason there were but few found to do such a thing. As a rule it was better for the children of men to have but a half-knowledge about the corpse-candle than to dare this thing, as few knew whether they could bear such a sight. But according to universal rule, " Every country nourishes brave men," and so it was in quiet Llanfihangel. A blacksmith of unusual stature and strength lived there, and his bravery and prowess had become a proverb throughout the country, and of his daring many things were spoken by the fireside. This smith took it into his head to go to the church porch every time a corpse-light was seen going towards the burial-ground. Through the advantage given him by his daring and courage, he was thus able to say beforehand who would be buried next, which appeared amazing to the people, because he invariably foretold the truth. At last was discovered what had been a mystery to the neighbours, and they knew that he was in the habit of going to the porch every time the corpse-light was seen, and that he there found out whose light it was.

On a certain night, as there were, according to custom, many men and boys in the smithy, their conversation turned to corpse-candles, and from talking to disputing hotly whether it was possible to know beforehand whose light it was. At last they asked the

smith for his opinion on the point, asking him
if it was true that he himself had acquired the
knowledge, to which he replied that it was
perfectly true.   Just then a neighbour entered
breathless and perspiring, having had a great
fright.   When he recovered himself a little,
he said he had seen a corpse-candle making
towards the churchyard, and if they went out
they could all see it.   Out they all went, and
there they saw the light approaching in the
direction of the burial-ground.   " Now then,"
said they to the smith, " go you to the porch this
'evening."   He answered that he was quite at
leisure and ready to go, and proud to be of use.
As the blacksmith's house and shop were at the
side of the churchyard, he had but a few steps
to take before finding himself amongst the
quiet inhabitants of the churchyard; so leaving his work as it was, away he went without
any hesitation to the church porch, so that he
might be there ready before the light came.
He was seen to enter the church, and very
soon the corpse-candle was seen coming along
the path, and then it, too, went into the porch.

After a little while the smith returned, looking
most unusually upset and frightened.   When
he was more collected, he related to the gathering what had happened.   He said he had gone
to the church porch, and after a short wait,
he saw the corpse-candle coming through the
churchyard and then to the church.   There,
standing as usual in the porch, was to be seen
the person who would be buried.   As the light

shone upon him, the smith recognised him as the Nanteos keeper. But as the corpse passed him by to enter the church, it turned towards him and exposed its grinning teeth in the most horrible and ghastly manner. He felt so alarmed that he was near to falling down dead, and indeed would so have fallen if he had not been a giant for strength. He said it was the last time he should go and see the corpse-light, to know who was going to die.

Some little time after this, the keeper was stricken by death in some form or other, and his body was brought to Llanfihangel to be buried, as the old smith had truly said. So the neighbours were assured that it was possible to identify the person whose light was seen, but that it was a great risk to life to seek to find out.

The next story gives a particularly unpleasant experience.

FOLLOWING HIS OWN CANDLE

It happened once that a young man of the neighbourhood of Ll——i went to visit a friend of his in the neighbouring district. After passing an amusing day, he had a mind to return, and of course his friend must go with him, to "send" his crony home.* As they

* To "send" any one means to go with him part of the way back—a Welsh idiom.

walked along talking of each other's affairs, they saw far off in front of them, a light. And one said to the other about it: " I tell you, that is a corpse-light, let's follow it and see whose light it is. Because they say you can see that, if you mind to get to the church-yard gate before the light goes through."

So away they went, and it was not long before they got to within measurable distance of the light. But as they followed, a great fear fell on the visitor, and he told his friend he could not go a step farther in pursuit. The other laughed in his face ; and so they separated. The friend went home, and left the man he had been visiting to follow the spirit of the light. He went on till he came to the church-yard entrance. There he plainly saw whose light it was. He went home dreadfully frightened, and took to his bed, from which he never rose again. He confessed to his family that he had seen *his own light* at the church-yard gate. But he never said a word as to its appearance, though it was supposed that the Thing had given him a ghastly look and nothing more. And very soon his funeral took place in the very churchyard where he had seen the light.

Mr. Davies now goes on to relate some

STORIES OF THE TOILI

Before passing on to stories of the Toili, a word of explanation regarding them may not be out of place, in case it happens that these lines travel to a region where there is no Toili, or fall into the hands of those not privileged to see it. The Toili was a spirit burial or funeral. It was also an apparition or "double"; and very often in days gone by one heard that So-and-so had seen his own apparition. In some parts the Cyheuraeth * was seen. The people of Glamorganshire always saw the Cyheuraeth; and the folks of Teify-side used to see, and still do see, the Toili. All the movement and action of a real funeral were to be perceived in the Toili. In this way the whole business of the real funeral could be known beforehand by the person who happened to witness the spectral one, and a few of his friends to whom he would speak about it. There was the crowd collected round a certain house, then came the corpse carried out to the bier or hearse, the reading, the prayers, the singing, and if any particularly penetrating voice were heard at the funeral in the crying of the deceased's relatives, that was sure to have been noticed beforehand in the Toili. In this way it came to be known very often which of a family was

* A horrible spectre, supposed to foretell death.

to go. In the movement of the procession the sound of the coach-wheels was loudly heard. And on it went, just like the real funeral, to the churchyard; there again it could be observed where the real body should be buried. The voice of the minister was clearly to be heard going through the burial service. As was the Toili, so was the funeral. But we have never heard of the church bell tolling for the Toili; that is the one difference between the vision and the reality.

They were able to predict the date of the burial from the time of night when the Toili appeared. If it were seen at the beginning of the night, the funeral would be soon; if very late at night, it would not happen quickly. Every one had his Toili, but it could not always be seen, and not by everybody. Those people born on Sunday could not see it, nor any other kind of spirit either.

As a rule we readily observed that whenever the Toili was heard or seen, a funeral did inevitably follow. And we only knew it fail once, thus showing there is no rule without exception.

It is interesting to read of this exception to an ordinarily fatal rule in the story called

THE TOILI WITHOUT A FUNERAL

Just as the Toili itself upsets the usual order of things, so we will reverse the general rule of writers by relating, first, the story of the Toili without a funeral. This case happened at a farm not very far from Tregaron, inhabited by a quiet and respectable old couple.   The dwelling-house was very old, and like other old things had become very fragile, but because the old man had been born and brought up in it, he had determined to end his days there also, on the old hearth so dear to him. But very suddenly he was taken ill with a high fever, which took hold of his system so powerfully that his improvement became very uncertain, and unless his constitution proved the stronger, there was little hope that he could pull through.   One night, when the fever was at its highest point, those who watched him were alarmed by a sudden and terrifying noise. They were two in number, sitting by the fireside ; and a little before midnight, after everybody else had gone to sleep, and when even the sick man seemed to be slumbering quietly, they heard this noise in the inner room where the patient was ; something like a great stove or furnace being raked out, they said.

At first they thought the invalid was awake, and had got out of bed in a state of unconsciousness and was knocking things about ; and they ran in, but everything was as usual, not a sign of anything having taken place there, so they came back. Whereupon they felt as if the door was open, and a multitude of people pushing in, and before they had time to speak, they found themselves in the midst of a crowd of men, without being able to move a step. *Yet nothing was to be seen.* Neither said a word to the other, perhaps overcome with fright, but both made the best of their way to the hearth and there sat down as close in the corner as they could. They could not hear a single word clearly, but only a sort of whispering all through the place, and felt perfectly sure they heard breathings. Presently it seemed that the place got clearer, and they heard men going out through the door, which in reality was shut and locked. At last they thought they heard a coffin closed in the next room. Therefore they knew that it was the Toili; and presently the coffin was taken up with great bustle and shaking—for the old man who was ill was very heavy—and then it was carried from the inner room, through the kitchen, knocking against the dresser as it went, for they distinctly heard the sound. Then it was taken outside, and there again they thought they heard the house door creak as the weight was forced against it. Then the coffin was put on the bier, and they heard the feet of those in the Toili moving away from the house.

Now there was no disputing that it really was the Toili, and so every one supposed there was no hope of recovery for the old man. But the wonderful thing is, that he got better! Then the point was, who was going to die? Weeks went by without a sign that Death had singled out any one of the family. Weeks ran into months, and years passed by without a single funeral from the place. Here was a mystery; the Toili followed by a burial was entirely natural, but a Toili without a funeral!! The best guess failed to solve the problem. However, the old house becoming at last in danger from the roof, it was necessary to build a new one, and the other fell to ruin, so that no burial ever could take place from there, and therefore quite naturally this unusual case of the Toili was explained.

I confess the explanation is hard to follow. It seems to suggest that apparently even destiny may be cheated on occasion, or perhaps the Toili in this case was an auto-suggestion.

The three stories that follow are very typical instances of the strange old belief.

THE UNBELIEVER AND THE TOILI

We were never very fond of that class of person who denies everything he cannot see through himself, and thinks it is impossible for anything to take place outside his own experience. . . . Such think themselves too wise to put trust in those foolish stories relating to spirits, corpse-candles, and such-like. They consider themselves too clever to listen to those kind of tales; but some even of that class are occasionally obliged to confess that there is a mystery about such coincidences which is beyond their understanding to comprehend. Of this class was the young man

who heard this Toili. He had publicly denied
the authenticity of spirits, and when he heard
any one relating a story of having seen one, he
would laugh in his face for superstition, and
contradict him in the most contemptuous
manner. Whether it was conceit, or whether
he did really consider himself wiser than the
common people, we do not know. But one
cold winter's night his head was brought low
and belief forced on him, in spite of his dis-
pleasure. . . .

In that part of the country—Teify-side—
they used to be very fond of "courting" of an
evening, and on "courting" nights the boys
would gather and go off together to the
different houses where their friends amongst
the maidens lived. On such a journey was the
young man when he heard the Toili. He had
a friend who was going to visit his sweetheart
some little way off, and our hero must needs go
with him for company. It was a frosty night,
and a thin covering of snow had fallen. They
had to cross Gors Goch on their way, and as
the bog was frozen, they got across with com-
parative ease. When they reached the farm,
the young man left his friend to go in and visit
his beloved, while he himself turned his steps
back across the Gors towards home. But on
the way there lived another friend, and to save
the trouble of calling up his own family to let
him in, he determined to stay with this friend
instead. Now this man lived in a cottage, in
a place where there were two or three other

workmen's houses. One of these was under the same roof as the friend's house, and in order to call on him, our young man had to pass the door of the upper house. . . . He hastened along as fast as his feet would carry him, for night was now rather far advanced, and very soon he came to the cottages. The next thing we know about him is, that he called up his friend, who let him in, and made a splendid fire to warm him. Then we find the friend observing that he trembled either from fear or cold, and looked terrified, which caused the question : "What has come to thee ! Art thou frightened ? "

At first he denied, and it was long before he let the cat out of the bag. But at last, hard pressed, he confessed that he *had* heard something he could not explain. "What didst thou hear ? Was it a spirit or the Toili ? " was immediately demanded. Now our friend did not know what to do, because he had always publicly scoffed at all such things, but here was his belief in himself collapsed without resistance. On the other hand, to keep silence might cause pain and trouble to his friend's family, who might fear he had heard something concerning them. At last he made an unequivocal confession of all that he had heard. . . . He said that all had gone well until he drew near the door of the cottage adjoining his friend's, and when opposite that house he thought he heard the sound of a man's voice speaking. Approach-

ing nearer, he recognised the voice at once
as that of the minister, the Rev. T. R., of
D——. He heard him take a certain text—
afterwards he remembered exactly what the text
was—and after the reading of the text, waited
to hear the beginning of the address. At
first he thought he was strong enough to
stop and listen to the sermon, but fear suddenly overcame him, and he left the door
and took refuge in the next house with his
friend. Besides, he felt almost too weak to
stand on his feet, or even shout to his friend, so
greatly had terror seized him. That was all he
had heard, but he had received proof enough of
the possibility of seeing and hearing the Toili,
and would deny it no longer.

In the house we have mentioned there lived
an old man and woman and their daughter,
all at that time in good health, considering
the age of the old people. But soon afterwards the wife was taken ill with jaundice,
and though every remedy was tried, she grew
weaker, and at last died of the complaint.
The day of the funeral came, but no preacher
could be found to read and pray by the door
when the corpse was carried out. All the
ministers in the neighbourhood had gone off
to the end of the county to attend some
monthly meeting that was being held that
week. Our young man, his friend and family,
waited with great interest to see if the real
funeral would take place like the Toili,
though it is true they were much puzzled as

to how it could happen, seeing that Mr.
T. R., the minister, was at the meeting.   But
on the morning of the day, as the young
man was himself on the way to the funeral,
he met the reverend pastor returning from
his journey, and although it took much per-
suasion, he finally induced him to come to
the funeral and do the service.   After reading,
praying, and hymn-singing, the minister chose
his text from the very same chapter and
verse as the young man had heard in the
Toili, and immediately began his address in
the same words as the ghostly sermon, well
remembered by the terrified listener, and
which now corroborated his account !

We have no hesitation in setting down
this old story as true, for we have not the
least doubt of the truthfulness of those who
told it to us—namely, the friend and family
of the young man himself.   We do not know
how it will appear to the wise and learned,
but we do know that it is not an easy task
to gainsay the facts of the case.

THE TOILI AT LLANBADARN ODWYN
CHURCHYARD

What we are about to chronicle happened
some years ago, during the time of September
harvest, and there are a number of people
living who were eye-witnesses of the circum-
stance.   Consequently it cannot have been

imagination, or anything of that kind, of which solitary individuals are sometimes accused when they see these inexplicable visions. There could have been no deception, as it happened in broad daylight, and on high and open ground, the season, as we have already observed, being harvest-time.

The cemetery and church of Llanbadarn Odwyn are situated on a high and healthy hill overlooking the beautiful little Vale of Aeron. Over against the church, on an equally salubrious spot, stands the farm called Birch Hill, more to the south than the church, but in sight of, and quite near it.   One day in harvest there happened to be a strong reaping party at Birch Hill, and they were reaping a field which overlooked the churchyard.   Just before noon, one of the men chanced to look that way, and perceived a funeral procession.   He remarked this to his fellow-labourers, and looking in the direction of the church, they one and all saw the funeral too.   It appeared to be rather different to the common run of burials, more " stylish," like that of a well-to-do person.   They particularly noticed a pall over the coffin, which was a very unusual thing with them.   The whole ceremony seemed to be taking place in perfect order.   Now the great question was, whose burial could it be?   They asked one another, but no one knew of any death within the district.   And at dinner-time they told the farmer's wife what they had seen, asking her if she knew what funeral it could be.   But

neither could she tell. However, those were
not the sort of people to be hindered from
finding out exactly what they wanted to know.
So they decided that the head-servant should
go to the sexton, and ask him whose burial
they had seen, and let them know on the
morrow. And at the proper time away went
the servant to the grave-digger to get the
information. But when he got there and asked,
not a sound or syllable of a funeral could he
hear of. The sexton was quite certain that
nobody had been buried that day, and said they
must have seen something else than a funeral.
The servant could not believe the sexton, who,
on the other hand, disbelieved the servant
when he asserted that he had seen a funeral
that day. And each one was so sure of his
own facts as to leave the matter a mystery
impossible to explain. The servant went home,
and when he said there had been no burial that
day at Llanbadarn it was concluded that they
must have seen the Toili, with which conclusion
the reapers also agreed on the morrow. Then
came the excitement of watching to see whose
funeral would follow. Some days later, as the
minister's family was returning home from
London for a stay in the country, it happened
that his wife was taken ill, and it was not long
before her soul left the body to join the world
of spirits. The family burial-place was at
Llanbadarn Odwyn, and no time was lost in
making arrangements for burying her there.
Every one was informed of the sad event, so

that on the day of the funeral quite a crowd of relations and family connections were gathered together to go and meet the corpse. And towards the time at which the Toili was seen, there was the real funeral in the cemetery, exactly in the same way as the phantom one was seen. Everything was the same, even to the white pall thrown over the coffin. So the reapers of Birch Hill were quite satisfied that it was the Toili of this funeral they saw, and no other. Here was an example of the Toili seen by a crowd of people in the broad light of noonday, each individual seeing it exactly in the same form in which the real funeral presently took place. Their eyes did not deceive them, because so many eyes perceived the same occurrence at the same moment, and moreover, the testimony of the sexton was certain proof that there was no burial in the churchyard that day. Let the wise explain that vision as they will.

THE TOILI OF RHOSMEHERIN

As already stated, night was the time when the Toili was commonly seen and heard. It was then one might expect to meet it, and men and women are to be found who have been carried along with it even to the churchyard gate. But the vision has been seen at midday and at the hour of dusk, and it was at this latter time that appeared the Toili of Rhosmeherin.

On a beautiful spring evening it happened
that a farmer, after a hard day's work, lingered
outside his house for a while, enjoying the soft
breeze that blew through wood and orchard,
and listening to the anthem of the winged
choir. Presently he chanced to look in the
direction of Bryn Meherin, where lived Vicar
Hughes, a well-known and industrious man in
his day ; and the farmer was amazed to perceive every appearance of a funeral there. He
knew very well that it could not be a funeral
either, for nobody was dead, and besides the
time of day was contrary to the usual hour for
burials, so he concluded that what he saw must
be the Toili. He called his family from the
house to look lest he should be mistaken. But
there, seen by all of them, was a complete
funeral, and from its appointments a very
respectable one. In front, preceding the crowd,
was a man on horseback ; then, according to
the custom of those parts, there followed the
men on foot, then the body. Over the coffin
was a black cloth. Then came the women on
foot, and last of all the coaches. As the procession moved slowly along a man on a white
horse from the crowd behind moved from his
place right up to the man on horseback at its
head.

Not a doubt remained with the spectators
that they had seen the Toili, and it was not
long before the vision was fulfilled. The
clergyman died soon afterwards, and on the
day of the funeral the farmer and family

observed carefully to see if it resembled the Toili.

The clergyman had always been greatly respected'; he was liked by all ranks and classes, and beloved by the poor; so that at the funeral there was a larger number of people than had ever been seen before. And there in their midst was a man on a white horse, who turned out to be one of the clergy, and who, anxious to be ready to take his part in the burial service, was seen to push forward from the back of the procession and move up to the front—exactly what had happened in the Toili.

We have heard that several other people also saw this Toili, and observed that the incidents of the real funeral were similar to those of the spectral one.

Really grisly was the belief in corpse-dogs, of which our author relates the following stories :

CORPSE-DOGS

Our "wrestlings with the spirits" have led us from corpse-candles to the Toili, and in natural order we now come to the subject of "corpse-dogs," not the least important of death omens. It is true that I have failed to get the knowledge of their appearance that I wanted, and can therefore not give a very good description of them. There are those I know that have seen corpse-candles, a spirit, and the Toili. But of the many tales concerning hell-hounds I have heard of but one person who actually saw one, and his free description must therefore suffice us. "Hell-hounds" is another name for these apparitions.

This particular corpse-dog was seen at a place called Llwyn Beudy Isaf by a member of the family who happened to be living there then, and that was about a hundred and fifty-two years ago. An inmate of the house was taken very ill one day, and at night the farm dog began to howl in a very unusual and disturbing manner. On the following night, as one of the sons of the family went out to look after the animals before going to bed, he heard a sound which he thought was made by a sheep or a pig coming towards him, with a curious noise of chains; he could hear a chain clanking quite plainly. As it came nearer him he saw the thing clearly, namely, a little dog in appearance, of a sort of reddish grey colour, dragging a chain. It ran past him with the speed of lightning, and he saw no sign of it again. He supposed some one had been leading it, but could see no one about. Directly afterwards their own dog began to howl in the most dismal and extraordinary way, and when this sound was heard all hope of recovery for the sick person was given up, and indeed it was not long before he drew his last breath.

The tradition about corpse-dogs is, that they are sent from hell to the country of the Earth to fetch corpses, and as a rule Death follows wherever they appear. And when they approach a dwelling where Death is coming they are seen by the dog of the house, and cause the animal such terror that it foams at the mouth, and utters dismal howlings as long as the hell-hounds continue near.

That is the reason why a dog howls before a death; when you hear that mournful sound you may be quite sure that a corpse-dog is in the neighbourhood, and if you observe which way the dog's head is turned, in that same direction is the demon animal. Some dogs are daring enough to go to the door of the sick person's house, where the corpse-dog watches —yes, and howl beneath the window of the room where Death awaits his prey. Although corpse-dogs are as a rule invisible, yet of their existence nobody has a doubt. That one has been actually seen by an individual is as good a proof as if a hundred or more had seen them. Dogs are reliable witnesses of their presence in any place where they come. They strike terror in any religious family, especially if any member of it be ill, and no small anxiety is felt until the foul creatures leave the neighbourhood, and the house-dogs cease to howl and foam. . . .

The hour of their visitation to a locality is generally towards the edge of night, just before cock-crow. Usually at that hour the dogs will begin howling in heart-rending fashion, as if pitying him who will soon be seized by the teeth of the hounds of hell, and find themselves gripped in the claws of the King of Terrors. As every reader must have heard many a dog howl, it would be idle to describe the sound which has often caused the remark, "We shall be sure to hear of a death very soon," and it is but rarely that it happens otherwise.

It is well known that dogs and horses are creatures gifted with very keen senses of scent and sight, especially after the shades of night have fallen on the face of Nature, and particularly as regards sight or smell of anything beyond the usual limits of this world, such as spirits, corpse-candles, Toili, hell-hounds and the like. But there is a great difference in the powers of individual dogs and horses in this respect. It is just the same with mankind; some have been endued with powers to behold the Unseen, while others again are found blind to every vision of the kind. That is the reason why it is useless to heed every dog that howls, but only certain ones in cases where it has been found that a death always follows their howling. . . . Such a one was old "Brins" of Tymawr, of respected memory. Shaggy and red-eyed, he was not a particularly good sheep-dog, but he was very faithful to his owners and full of doggish common sense. The voice of Brins always struck terror into the community, for well was it known that some one was sure to die if Brins opened his mouth to howl at night. People would go out and look to see in what direction his head was pointed, so as to know whereabouts the death would be.

There was an old butcher who had exceeded the allotted span of human days by ten years. At last his time came; he was taken ill, and from the hour when he began to keep to his bed, the old dog Brins began to howl. As night after night went by, John Hughes growing weaker and weaker, so did the dog continue his howlings. At first he gave tongue near his own home, but as the old man's end drew near, Brins went over to his house, the two places not being far apart. At last, such was his boldness that he crept right under the window of the room where the dying man lay, and howled steadily until the end came. After this his voice was not heard again at night, until just before another death occurred.

It was indeed bold of the old dog to go and howl beneath the sick man's window; because the wise who know say that as Death approaches, the Cŵn Annŵn (hell-hounds) draw round the house, and on the last night they enter the room and stay by the bedside, so as to be near when the breath leaves the body.

CHAPTER VII

WELSH FAIRIES

"Heaven defend me from that Welsh fairy."

READERS must not turn up their noses when they read the title of this short chapter. Of course nobody believes in fairies nowadays, but in the olden time most Welsh people did, and in other things more remarkable even than " y Tylwyth Teg," * such as giants and dragons. I could relate a most interesting story of a giant who once lived (rather long ago!) only about three miles from my own home; and there is a respectable tradition of a terrible dragon having been seen—history omits the date—flying over the town of Newcastle Emlyn. And I feel this volume would be incomplete without a passing reference to one of the most picturesque and romantic of the ancient Welsh beliefs. Sir John Rhys, the great Celtic scholar, has said almost the last word on the subject of Welsh fairy-lore, and there are indeed few crumbs of information that he neglected to gather about the Fair Folk. But I do not think he

* Literally, " Fair Family."
159

gleaned the two or three genuine fairy-tales which I found in Mr. Lledrod Davies' little pamphlet, and which I have translated, and will repeat here. For as folk-lore it is material far too valuable to be lost in a publication already out of print, and in any case inaccessible to people not conversant with the Welsh language. Personally I have only come across two people who had anything to say about the Tylwyth Teg, and they were not of the peasantry, but persons of antiquarian tastes, who had noted the instances they referred to as curiosities of local belief. So, though I have heard numbers of tales relating to superstitions such as corpse-candles, the Toili, &c., yet I have never myself heard a single *first-hand* story about fairies, and I fancy their disappearance from their old haunts dates very nearly from the time that Board Schools were established in Wales. Education then became—and very properly so—a practical and rather material business; children were told that fairies were "silly," in fact, non-existent, and so they learnt to despise the wonderful tales their parents and grand-parents knew, and would listen no more to them. So the old stories, handed down by word of mouth through centuries, and always greedily heard, and willingly remembered, were gradually forgotten; and as the elder folk died out, were nearly all lost. A pity, for trivial and even childish as they would sound to us who live in a world of scientific

wonders that those old people could never
dream of, and no longer require to feed our
imagination with the marvellous and supernatural, still all those ancient beliefs, legends
and superstitions always seem to me like the
romance of life crystallised, and, as such, a
very precious thing. For Romance and
Glamour grow rare as the world grows older,
though most of us have had a glimpse—even
though a momentary one—of what those two
names mean. And the power to express them
grows less; I think most people will agree
about that. But these old fairy beliefs and
curious traditions seem to transmit the true,
romantic atmosphere throughout the ages,
bringing to our knowledge what our forefathers thought and felt in that set of ideas
not immediately affected by their material
necessities and circumstances. So that is why
I think almost any of these old tales are
interesting and worth preserving.

W. Howells, who wrote that entertaining old
book, "Cambrian Superstitions," to which I have
often referred, has a great deal to say about
Fair Folk, or Ellyllyn, or Bendith eu Mammau,
for by these different names were the fairies
known in different districts. This is what he
tells us of their origin: "The following is
the account related in Wales of the origin of
the fairies, and was told me by an individual
from Anglesey. In our Saviour's time there
lived a woman whose fortune it was to be
possessed of near a score of children . . . and

L

as she saw our blessèd Lord approach her
dwelling, being ashamed of being so prolific,
and that He might not see them all, she concealed about half of them closely, and after
His departure, when she went in search of
them, to her surprise found they were all
gone.   They never afterwards could be discovered, for it was supposed that as a punishment from heaven, for hiding what God had
given her, she was deprived of them ; and, it
is said, these her offspring have generated the
race of beings called fairies.

Howells also mentions the interesting belief
formerly prevailing in Pembrokeshire and Carmarthenshire concerning mysterious islands,
inhabited by fairies, who "attended regularly
the markets at Milford Haven and Laugharne,
bought in silence their meat and other neces-
saries, and leaving the money (generally silver
pennies) departed, as if knowing what they
would have been charged.   They were sometimes visible and at other times invisible.   The
islands, which appeared to be beautifully and
tastefully arranged, were seen at a distance
from land, and supposed to be numerously
peopled by an unknown race of beings.   It was
also imagined that they had a subterraneous
passage from these islands to the towns."

Our author tells us that both Cardiganshire
and Carmarthenshire were specially favoured
by the Tylwyth Teg ; he heard of them on the
banks of the Gwili (a tributary of the Towy),
where "they made excursions to the neigh-

bouring farms to inspect the dairies, hearths, barn-floors, and the ' ystafell,' * to reward the meritorious housemaid, and to punish the slut and sluggard. It is said they were not partial at all to the Gospel, and that they left Monmouthshire on account of there being so much preaching, praying to, and praising God, which were averse to their dispositions."

It seems that there was a well-known tradition in Carmarthenshire about one Iago ap Dewi, a man, Howells tells us, of considerable talent, who translated the "Pilgrim's Progress" into Welsh. He lived in the parish of Llanllawddog, and " was considered a wonderful man and of great learning, as he spent the whole of his time in study and meditation; that he was absent from the neighbourhood for a long period, and the universal belief among the peasantry was, that Iago got out of bed one night to gaze on the starry sky, as he was accustomed (astrology being one of his favourite studies), and whilst thus occupied the fairies, who were accustomed to resort to the neighbouring wood, passing by, carried him away, and he dwelt with them seven years. Upon his return he was questioned by many as to where he had been, but he always avoided giving them a reply." Howells afterwards goes on to say that others with whom he conversed related that " their parents credited the above story, and that they had no question of the existence of fairies and their wonderful exploits; but one

* Rooms.

Mary Shon Crydd said that when a child she knew the daughter of Iago ap Dewi, and that she thought it very probable that he had been from home with some learned characters, but the superstition of the people led them to attribute his learning, &c., to the interference of the fairies." Although it disposes of the fairy idea, " Mary Shon Crydd's " explanation of Iago's absence, though prosaic, was, I should think, the true one ! But it is interesting to read of such a tradition being extant in days so comparatively near our own.

All dwellers in the country are familiar with the appearance of " fairy rings," those curious and inexplicable circles that occur in the grass of meadows and lawns. No amount of mowing obliterates them, and probably nothing short of digging up or ploughing would get rid of them. In Wales these odd patches seem to have ever been regarded with a mixture of fear and interest, as the undoubted haunts of the Twlwyth Teg, and were carefully shunned in consequence, especially after nightfall. Howells says, regarding these rings, that " no beasts will eat of them, although some persons suppose that sheep will greedily devour the grass." He adds that he had a friend who told him that when he was a child he was always warned by his mother never to approach, much less enter, the rings, for they were enchanted ground, and anybody going near them was liable to be carried off by the Fair Folk. In connection with the fairies' practice of kidnap-

ping human beings, there are many stories in
"Cambrian Superstitions," most of which have
one feature in common, namely, that when the
people thus carried off returned to this upper
world—in the cases where they did return, but
that did not always happen—they always
supposed they had been but a few moments
absent, though the period had often run into
years, as in Iago ap Dewi's case.

Giraldus Cambrensis, in his "Itinerary
through Wales," in the twelfth century, heard
many marvels, and not the least of these was
the tale of one Elidorus, a priest, who in his
youth had been carried off by the fairies, and
by them held in captivity for many years.
According to Giraldus, he made some use of
his time amongst them by learning their
language, which he is said to have told the
Bishop of St. David's much resembled the
Greek idiom!

I will now proceed with Mr. Lledrod Davies'
account of the Tylwyth Teg, as he heard of
them in Cardiganshire, not so very many
years ago.

"In collecting and noting down these few
tales from an older generation, it is useless to
try and trace their source in the history of the
old times before ours.   It is enough for readers
to know now that there were, always 'little
people' of that kind in Wales, and that our
ancestors were very sociable and friendly with
them.   I take the following tales from some I

heard by word of mouth in the country of Teify-side.

"Small of stature were the Tylwyth Teg, towards two feet in height, and their horses of the size of hares. Fair of aspect were they, and very fine their clothing; their clothes were generally white, but on certain occasions they are said to have been seen dressed in green; their gait was lively, and ardent and loving was their glance. Very mischievous if thwarted, kind and good-natured otherwise. And—speaking from the human point of view—they were thieves by inclination, and therefore it was considered rather dangerous to have them coming round houses, as they regarded all property as shared in common. . . .

They were peaceful and kindly amongst themselves, diverting in their tricks, and charming in their walk and dancing. They were good-natured to good-natured people, and hateful to those who hated them. They were subterranean people, therefore in the earth was their home. There were their country, their cities, and their castles, and there lived their King. And from thence they made their incursions into the Earth-country, in some way that nobody can guess or know, nor is there any hope of any one ever knowing."

Our author goes on to information about the fairy rings, and has two stories to relate of people who disappeared in them.

THE FAIRY RINGS

A number of these rings are shown by the old people all through the country; I myself remember many of them. They were of various appearance; sometimes the circle was but small, again others were seen as large as a mill-wheel. . . . These rings were the places where the Tylwyth Teg came to dance on fine, bright nights. The circles were only to be seen on marshy meadow-ground, and sometimes on hay land. On a moonlight night was the time to see these rings, because then the fairy folk came out of their hiding-places to whirl and dance about; and so they may be seen until the Son of the Dawn* opens his eyes and causes them to disappear. On the following morning the keen-eyed may see the mark of their feet on the meadow. The grass that surrounds the rings is thicker than the rest, because no animal will feed on the spot where the fairies have been. So these circles remained by day as the Tylwyth Teg had shaped them; and they were considered places it was best to keep away from, except in broad daylight while the owner of cattle was always alarmed if he saw his animals go near them. There was great danger in approaching the rings when the Fair Folk were dancing; for there was such magic in their melody, such allurement in their appearance, and such an

* *I.e.*, the sun.

attraction in their whirling, that it was impossible for any one who came near to resist their charm. If within their enchanted circle they could entice a handsome youth, or a pure maiden, nevermore would they be seen in this world. In some cases people have been kidnapped accidentally and against their will.

Such a one, and who lived with them for a year, was the servant of Allt Ddu. This farm stood half-way along the road between Pontrhydyfendigaid and Tregaron. It is said that this servant and another one left the house at dusk to look for some cattle—yearlings and two-year-olds—that had strayed that morning. . . . So, as was natural to do in such a case, one servant took one road and his companion the other, so as to be sure of coming across them. But after hours spent in searching, one of the men returned; how he found the cattle is not related, but at least they came back in safety. And as it was very late—indeed nearly morning—he felt anxious about the safety of his fellow-servant, as he was afraid some accident had befallen him in one of the bog-holes of Gors Goch. Morning came but no servant, and not a sound of his footsteps returning. Then inquiries were made, but no sign or syllable could be heard of him. Days and weeks passed by, and now, doubt arose about his fate amongst his relations, for they began to suspect that his fellow-servant was the cause of his disappearance, and had murdered him and concealed his body. So the other labourers, night after night, accused the poor man of the crime; and though the young fellow protested his innocence in the most emphatic manner, yet appearances were against him; he could not satisfy their doubts, and a black mark stood against his name. At last, whatever happened, he determined to go to a "wise man" (a person of uncommon importance in those days) and ask him point-blank if he could tell what had happened. So he went, and laid the case before the "wise man," who told him that his companion was alive, but that a year and a day must elapse before they would see him again, and that then they must seek him at the very hour when he was lost.

So, after weary waiting, a year and a day passed by, and the long-expected hour arrived. And then the missing man's family, with the servant at their head, betook themselves to the appointed glade; and there, to their amazement, whom should they see in the midst of a fairy ring, dancing as gaily and happily as any one, but the lost youth. Then, according as the wise man had directed, his fellow-servant seized him by his coat collar and dragged him away, saying to him, "Where hast thou been, lad?"

The other replied, "Hast thou got the cattle?" He thought he had been at that spot only two or three minutes. When it was explained to him that he had been in

the fairy ring, and how he had been stolen
by them, he said they had been such good
company that he never supposed he had been
more than a few minutes with them. And
great was the joy at recovering the lost
one.

THE MAIDEN WHO WAS LOST IN A
FAIRY RING

I will only tax the reader's patience with
two of the tales about these fairy rings,
because we come across such tales in various
forms all through the country. But the
extraordinary case of the disappearance of
the maiden in this story is excuse enough, I
think, for introducing it into this book of
memories.

In an old farm on Teify-side there lived a
very respectable family; and in order to
carry on the work of the farm briskly they
kept both men and maid servants. On a
certain evening a servant man and maid went
out to fetch the cattle home for milking, and
all of a sudden the man lost sight of the
maid, and, although he searched and called,
no sign of her or sound of her voice reached
him. He went back with the cows, and told
the family of the mysterious disappearance
of the girl. From the evil reputation that
the Tylwyth Teg had in those parts, it was

decided to consult a "wise man" at once. Away they went to him, and after answering the usual inquiries he said the girl had been snatched into the fairies' ring and that she was with them now. If they were careful they might get her back after a year and a day, if they would go to the appointed place at the proper time.

All was done as the wise man directed, and great was their astonishment to perceive the maiden dancing away in the midst of the Fair Folk, and, as they were instructed, they seized and drew her out of the magic circle, happy and in good health.

Her master was told by the wise man to be careful never to touch her with iron after she was rescued. At first he was very particular about this, but as time went on they all got careless, and at last one day, just as she had dressed to go on an errand, he accidentally touched her with a horse's bridle; when, as suddenly as pulling a cat out of the fire, he entirely lost sight of the maid. He rushed off at once to the wise man for help, but was told that the girl was gone never to return. We may observe further, in this connection, that it was formerly supposed that the Tylwyth Teg always hovered round about dwelling-houses watching people, especially at night. And in all likelihood, according to this story, they had kept an eye on the maiden ever since she was taken away from them.

THE TIME OF THEIR DANCING

The fairies' dancing took place when spring began, and continued throughout the summer. But spring, as a rule, was the season of their merriment, and at that time children would be lost, yes, and people of full age too. Readers will surely have heard these tales of children being stolen and returning again after some years; of the frequent visitation by the Tylwyth Teg of families in a neighbourhood, of their boldness as winter began, and their anger if every family were not careful to put money, food, and such things in convenient places near the hearth, so that when the fairies came they could take what they wanted without difficulty. They required great cleanliness of every woman and girl they met with. If care was not taken in these respects, their curse was sure to fall on the family, in years to come. Night was the time when they visited the earth, and from midnight till morning they enjoyed themselves frolicking about hay-fields and marsh-lands.

They were very sociable beings. So much so that it was with difficulty they were got rid of once they got their heads into the houses of any neighbourhood. The only way to get rid of them was to throw rusty iron at them. To do this was like spitting in the face of God, the greatest insult you could hurl at them. Away they went at once, never to return except for deeds of vengeance. . . .

It may be observed, amongst their other characteristics, that they only inhabited certain parts of the country. The neighbourhood of Swydd Ffynon was especially distinguished by them. All around there would be seen the "rings" on every fine morning in spring and summer, while other parts of Wales were entirely ignorant of these fairy circles, and never a sign or sight of them was to be had.

THE FAIRY OINTMENT

In the quiet village of Swydd Ffynon there lived an old woman who died about twenty years ago, when drawing near her hundredth year. She was very fond of old stories ; in a word, she simply lived on them. She was in her element when relating ancient tales of the adventures of the Welsh folk, and according to her they were full of adventures in those days. And amongst others, she told the following story about her grandmother : This grandmother when young, seems to have been a pious and thoughtful person, very fond of the society of invisible beings, and the inhabitants of the spirit-world. Also, by some means or other, she got into communication with the Fair Folk, and became great friends with them ; her hearth became a kind of rendezvous for them ; and so faithful was she to them that she thoroughly gained their favour and confidence, such a thing as seldom happens to human beings. So fond of her were they that they invited her to go with them to one of their palaces under the earth, to which she heartily consented. When she got there she found herself in the most beautiful and stately house her eyes had ever seen ; in truth, never had she imagined such a place was possible. How she went there she did not know ; all she knew was that she had left the Earth country, and was now an inhabitant of a region she had not dreamed could exist ; but she went there and returned in some way entirely unknown to herself. .

At last one day she found herself summoned to the fairy country on an errand as nurse to the wife of one of their princes, who lived in a palace magnificent to a degree that exceeds earthly language to express. There were splendid ornaments, costly pearls, a golden pavement, partitions hung with silks of varying hue, and the garments of the people all changing white and blue. Indeed the old woman was puzzled to describe the splendours of the house, clothes and so on. There was installed the nurse, and her charge, the fairy infant, slept on a bed of down, with coverings of the finest lawn. Everything she wanted was complete and at hand. The nurse was amazed at such perfection, and astonished that a person like herself should have been summoned by such princely people.

While tending the baby night and morning, she had to anoint him with a certain ointment. When this ointment was given her, she was told to be careful not to let it touch the eyes, as it was injurious and even destructive to the sight. At first her fear of the ointment caused her to be very careful in using it, but as time went by she grew forgetful. So in a little while, as she was anointing the infant one day, something accidentally tickled her eye, and at once her hand, faithful to its owner, went up to the eye and rubbed it gently. Immediately it was as if a veil fell from her eyes, and she began to see things a thousand times more wonderful than before. In the course of the day she saw many a marvellous and splendid vision. She saw the Fair Folk quite plainly, little men and women, going and coming through the palace, and carrying presents of every kind to her lady. No lack of dainties was brought her, the purest kindness and affection were displayed. Later on, when undressing the child, she remarked to the princess on the number of visitors she had had that day.

"How do you know that?" asked the princess, "have you anointed your eyes with the ointment?" And in the flash of an eyelid she leapt from her couch, and striking one hand with the other, she blew on the nurse's eyes, which immediately lost sight of the enchanted surroundings, and though she tried hard in future days, nevermore did she see the princess, or any of the fair family or their doings.

And so, without knowing how, she found herself by her own fireside at home, just as usual, and that was the last of her stories about the Tylwyth Teg. And I also leave them here, for though I could add other stories to these I have noted, I have written enough about them now. I knew the old woman who told this story, and she always insisted she was the grandchild of the fairies' nurse, and, moreover, was very proud of the fact, and not without cause either.

I should have mentioned earlier that in translating Mr. Lledrod Davies' tales, I have left the names of places exactly as he had them. Where they are filled in they are the real ones, several of them places I know. It will be noticed that he often makes use of the expression "Teify-side." Now that name we generally apply to the district of the lower Teify, lying more or less between the towns of Llandyssil and Cardigan. But from what Mr. Davies says, he evidently includes in this term all the upper valley of the Teify too, which rises in the hills not many miles away from his native village, and most of his stories are located more or less in that neighbourhood. It is, or was until late years, a remote and lonely district, backed by the wild moors of the Ellineth Mountains, that to this day look as if they might be the last refuge of all the fairies, ghosts, and goblins of Wales. With these mountain wastes behind, and the gloomy stretch

of the great Tregaron bog before them, is it
any wonder that the imaginative Celtic inhabitants of Pontrhydyfendigaid and the surrounding hamlets saw, and wished to see, evidences of
the supernatural in almost every unimportant
coincidence? To them it came natural to
believe in those

> " Faery elves,
> Whose midnight revels, by a forest-side,
> Or fountain, some belated peasant sees,
> Or dreams he sees, while overhead the moon
> Sits arbitress."

George Borrow tells us that when he was
walking through Cardiganshire, he came one
evening to a large sheet of water not far from
Tregaron. He must needs find out the name
of this little lake, and therefore knocked at
the door of a cottage that happened to be close
by, in order to ask the information. A woman
opened the door, of whom Borrow seems to
have asked a great many tiresome questions,
after his usual habit; but this time he elicited
the curious information from his victim that
a fairy cow was supposed to live in the lake,
a " water-cow, that used to come out at night,
and eat people's clover in the fields." That
odd tradition was living only sixty years ago,
which is interesting to think of.

Now I have told the little I have been able
to gather about the Tylwyth Teg and their
ways, and so we will bid them farewell, and
turn to more serious subjects.

M

CHAPTER VIII

WISE MEN, WITCHES, AND FAMILY CURSES

"Wizards that peep and that mutter."

WHEN reading a provincial daily paper a few days ago, I came across the following paragraph :

"Although the school-master has been abroad in Wales for quite a long time, the belief in witchcraft still lingers here and there, and cropped up yesterday in an assault case at Aberavon, where one woman accused another of 'marking her house with a criss-cross to bewitch her.'"

It seems curious to read these words in the twentieth century, and it is hard to realise that a very few generations ago the woman who had put the "criss-cross" on her neighbour's house would have stood a very good chance of losing her life by being ducked by the mob for a witch, if indeed legal proceedings had not been taken against her.

As late as the year 1664 the great judge, Sir Matthew Hale, presided at the trial which resulted in the condemnation and hanging of two poor women as witches, and the last execution of the kind took place in 1682 when

three other wretched women were executed at
Exeter for the same offence, on their own
confession. And the statute against witchcraft passed under James the First was not
repealed until the reign of George the Second,
though by that time it was indeed practically
a dead letter. Mental progress and education
have since done their part in abolishing that
panic fear of witchcraft which, supported by a
bad law, caused the persecution and death of
so many innocent persons for more than a
century; but that belief—genuine if surrep-
titious—in the powers of "wise" men and
women still lingers in the minds of the people
in the West Country, one need only live in
Wales for a few years to find out.

Nor must one feel too scornful of such "superstition" when one recollects how palmists,
clairvoyants, and crystal-gazers flourish in
London and every other city on the payments
of hundreds of well-educated and enlightened
people. "Oh, a pack of silly women with more
money than sense," you may exclaim. To
which I reply, "Not at all," if the testimony of
a most respectable fortune-teller who was once
well known to me can be believed. According
to her, quite a number of her clients belonged
to the sterner (and we presume) more sensible
sex, and my own observation has also led me to
conclude that men on the whole are quite as
much tempted to peer into futurity as women
are, only naturally they think it their duty to
pretend indifference on such matters! Still,

however that may be, the Bond Street fortune-
teller, with whom one makes a solemn appointment, and who never " looks at a hand " under
a guinea, is nevertheless but a witch, belonging
to the same ancient guild as the unkempt old
woman who lives in a hovel on the sea-shore
near a certain little town in Cardiganshire.
This particular old woman has quite a local
reputation as a witch—even attaining to the
fame of having her portrait on a postcard—and
is much resorted to by summer visitors who
wish to have their fortunes told.

But Cardiganshire, especially the Northern
part, has always been a stronghold of belief in
witches and wise men, and their supposed
powers of putting a " curse " on the persons or
property of those who annoyed them.   There
is a story told of an old woman who had the
reputation of being a witch in a lonely
district of the wild hills of North Cardiganshire.
She was on the road one day, when the doctor
came riding along in great haste, whom she
tried to detain.   But he, either not understanding what she wanted, or unwilling to
stop, urged his horse forward, somewhat roughly
bidding the old crone begone.   Shrieking after
him, she told him to beware, " as she would
lay a curse upon his horse," which threat he
soon forgot, and after visiting his patient
returned home in safety.   That night, however,
Dr. G. was roused from his sleep by the groom,
who asked him to come out at once to the
horse, as it seemed to be very ill.   To make

the story short, the poor animal died in a few hours' time, nor could its owner ever determine the nature of its extraordinary attack, as it was apparently perfectly well when stabled for the night. But the coincidence between the horse's death and the witch's words was certainly striking.

I am reminded of another and quite modern instance of a Welsh witch's curse, though to avoid localisation I will not say exactly where she lived in the Principality. Her father was cowman at a house called Fairview, inhabited by a family called Trower. Mr. Trower possessed a rather savage bull, which one day broke loose, charged all who tried to catch him, and finally, sad to relate, gored and killed the poor cowman. He had lived in a cottage on the estate, and nothing could exceed the kindness and sympathy shown by the Trower family to his daughter in her bereavement. We will call her Patty Jones. After a decent interval had elapsed, Mr. Trower gave the woman notice to quit, as the cottage was wanted for somebody else. Although every indulgence regarding the notice was given, and continual consideration shown, Patty, being a woman of violent and ungrateful temper, took the matter very badly. She refused to go, and was eventually evicted, and her goods sold. It is said that meeting Mr. Trower on the road one day, she took the occasion to call down the wrath of Heaven upon him and his family, and made no secret afterwards of having "put a

curse " upon her benefactors, for such indeed
the Trowers had shown themselves. Whether
it is ever really given to any human being so
to blast the lives of fellow-creatures or not, one
cannot tell. But it is certain that this particular family thereafter appeared for some years
to be singled out by fate for more than their fair
share of ill-luck, though, to avoid recognition,
further details must not be given here.

At the sale of her goods a man named
Morgan happened to buy Patty Jones's cow.
Whereupon she told him she would "put a
curse " on the animal, so that "he would never
get any good from her." Sure enough, soon
afterwards the cow sickened with a mysterious
complaint, which defied the skill of the local
" cow-doctor." So Morgan, advised by his
neighbours, went to seek counsel of a "white
witch," who gave him a charm which she said
would cure the cow. "And now," she added,
" wouldn't you like me to put a curse on that
woman? Because I can if you wish it." But
Morgan magnanimously replied, "Oh, no. *I do
not wish* her any harm whatever," and departed
with his charm and cured his cow. It would
be interesting to know the nature of this
" charm," whether it was a written form of
incantation, or something of the nature of a
medicine. Mr. Henderson, whose interesting
book on folk-lore I have already quoted, tells
us of a piece of silver at Lockerby in Dumfries-
shire, called the Lockerby Penny, which was
used against madness in cattle. It was put

into a cleft stick, and the water of a well stirred round with it, after which the water was bottled off and given to any animal so afflicted. In other districts certain pebbles and stones are supposed to have the same magic property.

Some Welsh witches are said to treat their patients with sulphur, a remedy which I think savours more of "black magic" than "white."

It seems that a favourite trick of North Cardiganshire witches was to "put a spell" on the pigs of any neighbour who annoyed them, making the poor animals *pranking* mad (as my informant expressed it). And nothing would cure this madness till the witch had been fetched, and (doubtless for a consideration) consented to remove the spell.

However, belief in the powers of "wise" men and women is now chiefly confined to their abilities as healers, and in this capacity they are still resorted to in the more remote districts of Cardiganshire. The cure—whatever the malady—appears to be always the same, and is called "measuring the wool." The witch takes two pieces of yarn—scarlet for choice—of exactly the same length. One of these is bound round the wrist or leg of the patient; the other is worn in the same way by the healer. The patient goes home, and after a few days the witch measures her own piece of yarn. If it has shrunk from the original length, well and good; the yarn continues to grow shorter (so it is said) and the patient

recovers. But if on the contrary the yarn
grows perceptibly slacker, the patient gets
worse and will surely die. The person who told
me about the bewitched pigs had also much
to say regarding this practice of "measuring
the yarn." She declared that quite lately
a friend of hers, a young man, who was very
ill with "decline" and for whom ordinary
doctors could do nothing, went at last to consult a "wise woman" in the parish of Eglwysfach * in North Cardiganshire. She measured
the yarn for him, and he immediately began
to recover and is now well and working at the
business which ill-health had forced him to
leave. In this case faith must have been a
strong factor towards recovery. But

> " I cannot tell how the truth may be ;
> I say the tale as 'twas said to me."

* "Eglwysfach" is the real name, and in "Welsh Folk-
lore" Mr. Owen relates a case of "measuring the yarn"
in the same village, where the custom seems to have been
long prevalent and firmly believed in. His account of the
charming for a case of "Clefyd y Galon" (or heart-sickness)
is worth quoting. The patient was bidden to roll his
sleeves up above the elbow, then "Mr. Jenkins (a respectable farmer and deacon amongst the Wesleyans) took a
yarn thread and placing one end on the elbow measured to
the tip of Felix's (the patient) middle finger, then he tells
his patient to take hold of the yarn at one end, the other
end resting the while on the elbow, and he was to take fast
hold of it, and stretch it. This he did and the yarn length-
ened, and this was a sign he was actually sick of heart-
disease. Then the charmer tied the yarn around the
patient's left arm above the elbow, and there it was left,
and in the next visit measured again, and he was pronounced
cured."

Only a year ago, in my own district, I heard of a young girl being taken to the local "wise man" to have "her wool measured," but in her case the charm does not seem to have worked well, as though she did not die, she is still ailing. Another wizard, who died only last year, was an old man who lived at Trawscoed in Cardiganshire. He also worked cures with scarlet worsted, and enjoyed a great local reputation.

The use of scarlet wool as a charm is of great antiquity, and is supposed to be originally derived from the practices of the magicians of Babylon. And according to Theocritus, the Greek maidens used it as a charm to bring back faithless lovers. Mr. Elworthy, in his book on the " Evil Eye," refers to the ancient use made of coloured yarn in incantations, quoting from Petronius : " She then took from her bosom a web of twisted threads of various colours, and bound it on my neck."

In South Wales, as in many other districts, witches were supposed to have the power of transforming themselves into hares. Especially, as I have said before, was this superstition rife in North Cardiganshire, and there to this day, any hare that has white about it is called " a witch hare," and it is held very unlucky to kill it, while until quite lately incidents such as the following were freely repeated and firmly believed among the shepherds, small farmers, and miners who composed the scanty population of those lonely hills.

One day, the story goes, a funeral party was proceeding from the deceased's house towards the churchyard, when suddenly a hare was seen running just ahead of the procession. Nobody took much notice of it at first, thinking it had merely been disturbed from its form, and would probably soon disappear on one side of the road or the other. There was neither hedge nor fence to prevent its doing so, for the road was only a mountain track, which the hare might have left at any moment to seek cover among the heather and fern of the hill-side. But this it did not do; to the astonishment of all, the animal, apparently not a whit frightened by the people behind, held steadily on its way. Sometimes, of course, owing to its swiftness, it would be lost to view for a few moments, but always a turn of the way would bring it in sight again, and so it led the procession to the burial-ground. Then on a sudden it vanished as mysteriously as it had appeared. For no man could say what direction it took; only that at one moment it was there in plain view of all, and at the next it was gone. And after that, nobody present doubted that the creature was no hare, but a witch in that shape, who, scenting the approach of Death, had added her noisome presence to the crowd of mourners, until their arrival on consecrated ground had forced her to fly.

There is a tale belonging to the same district —roughly speaking—of which I have unfortunately only heard the vague outlines, but the incident is worth relating even without details, as it seems extraordinary in whatever way it is explained.

On a certain day, not very many years ago, a hare was hunted somewhere in the hill-country bordering the shires of Montgomery and Cardigan. From all accounts, never was better sport seen; the animal was game to the last, and by many a twist and turn managed to cheat its pursuers. At last, however, it appeared exhausted; the hounds closed in, and the hunters, immediately behind, saw them hurl themselves upon their quarry. The huntsman hastened forward, and every one pressed round to see the gallant animal which had given such a splendid run. But where was the hare? Whimpers and yelps of disappointment from the hounds proclaimed that their prey had escaped, but the question was, how? No hare that ever lived could have eluded the hounds as they fairly threw themselves upon her, but still the fact remained, "Puss" had disappeared, vanishing somehow in the very onslaught of tearing, eager hounds, and before the eyes of several spectators. Of course the story in the country has ever been that a "witch hare" was hunted that day, and "every one knows" that nothing but a silver bullet can destroy a witch.

The belief that only a silver bullet can harm a witch is illustrated in my next story. It was related to me by the Rector of a certain parish in Pembrokeshire, who said that though the people it concerned had been dead some years, the incident was still repeated with conviction by the country-folk of the district.

There was an old woman living in the village of Llaw——n who was supposed to be a witch and to have the power of changing herself into a hare. It was asserted that she had often been seen in this guise, and several persons tried on various occasions to shoot the uncanny beast. But no shot would touch it. However, "John the Smith" was a cunning man, and one day he loaded his gun with a silver sixpence in lieu of shot, and went out to look for the "witch hare." Presently he came across it in a field, and then —Bang! went his gun. Instantly the poor animal made off, but the sixpence had evidently found its mark, for as the hare ran it trailed a hind leg behind it. Still, lame as it was, it managed to elude the smith, and, turning in the direction of the village, disappeared. But that evening John went to the house of 'Liza the Witch, and, knocking at the door, cried, "How be'st thou, 'Liza?"

"John, John, thou very well knowest how I be," was the reply. Nor would she allow him to enter. Then John the Smith went home well satisfied that he had done what no one else had been able to do, and had wounded the "witch hare."

Apropos of this belief in a witch's powers of self-transformation, a rather curious incident came under my notice in my own neighbourhood some few months ago. Two gentlemen were partridge-shooting, and in the course of their walk the path they followed should have led them through the garden of a somewhat lonely cottage inhabited by an old woman. This woman was known to be very unpopular with her neighbours, in consequence, it was supposed, of a quarrelsome disposition. When the shooters reached this cottage, they found, to their surprise, that the gate by which they usually passed through the premises was fastened with a padlock. A shout produced the old woman from the house, who hastened to let them through, apologising profusely for the padlock, but saying she had been obliged to lock her gate, because "the boys were so bad to her. Look," she added, pointing to the end wall of her cottage, that is what they did to me last night." And there, nailed to the wall, was a black rabbit. One of the gentlemen, to cheer her, said jokingly, "Oh, that's nothing. A black rabbit! Isn't that lucky?" "No," was the answer, "not lucky; very bad luck, and they knew that very well."

To any one conversant with Cardiganshire superstitions, there is no doubt that the nailing up of the black rabbit was intended to signify that the inhabitant of the house

was a witch.   True, the animal should have
been a hare, but the Ground Game Act having
caused hares to become almost extinct in this
district, the perpetrators of the insult took the
best substitute they could find in the shape of
the black rabbit, well knowing that its sinister
significance would not be lost on the poor
old woman.

To return for a moment to the Pembrokeshire
village we have already mentioned, Llaw———n,
where there is a beautiful ruin of a castle, most
picturesquely situated on the edge of a wooded
cliff overhanging the river Cleddau.   In olden
times this castle was a place of great importance as a Palace of the Bishops of St. David's,
some of whom, it is said, preferred its strong,
well-fortified walls to their splendid palace in
the episcopal city.   And in Llaw———n Castle
there was once imprisoned a celebrated witch,
Tanglost ferch Glyn, against whom the reigning prelate, Bishop John Morgan, had taken
proceedings for some rather serious offence, and
whom he pronounced " accursed," or, in other
words, excommunicated.   After escaping once
from custody, and being rearrested, Tanglost
made submission, and (we presume) did penance,
and was at length released, though banished
from the diocese of St. David's.   Thereupon
she betook herself to Bristol, where, engaging
the services of another witch, one Margaret
Hackett, she endeavoured to " distrew " her
enemy the Bishop by witchcraft.   After a
time, Tanglost ventured to return to Pem-

brokeshire, and at a certain house * (still well known and inhabited), "in a chambre called Paradise Chambre," made, with Hackett's help, two waxen images for injuring the Bishop. Two images not being powerful enough to do the work, Tanglost and her coadjutor called in the aid of a third party, "which they thought hadde more counynge and experience than they had, and made the IIIrd ymage to distrew the Bishop." However, not only did the prelate continue to live and flourish, but, as was inevitable, knowledge of these sinister designs reached his ears, and Tanglost, with her two assistants, was summoned to appear for judgment before the Prior of Monckton, who held jurisdiction in her neighbourhood. Escaping for the moment, she again fled to Bristol, but was there reached by the long arm of the Church, and arrested on a charge of heresy. Four Doctors of Divinity considered her case, and handed her over to the Bishop for punishment, which would probably have meant being burnt as a witch in the

* Perhaps this house had an ancient reputation for possessing an atmosphere suitable for such "works of darkness." For Giraldus Cambrensis, writing three hundred years before the time of Tanglost, mentions it as being haunted by an unclean spirit which "conversed with men, and in reply to their taunts upbraided them openly with everything they had done from their birth, and which they were not willing should be known by others . . . the priests themselves, though protected by the crucifix or the holy water, on devoutly entering the house were equally subject to the same insults. . . ."

market-place, if Fate had not again interfered through the efforts of her friends, who caused Tanglost to be arrested on an accusation of debt, bailed her successfully out of prison, and rescued her from the Bishop's emissaries. Then a bill in Chancery was filed against her, praying that the Mayor and Sheriffs of the city of Bristol should be ordered to arrest her, and bring her before the King in Chancery. But to make a long story short, Tanglost, who seems to have been a woman of infinite resource, managed once more to evade this fresh danger, and it is to be supposed eventually died in her bed, in spite of her unlawful traffic with witchcraft. Her persecutor, Bishop John Morgan, held the See of St. David's from 1496 to 1505, and reference to the Chancery proceedings against Tanglost are to be found at the Record Office under " Early Chancery Proceedings."

The practice of making waxen images of the person to be injured is of immemorial antiquity. We read in Professor Maspero's " Dawn of Civilisation " about the Egyptian magicians that " to compose an irresistible charm they merely required a little blood from a person, a few nail-parings, some hair, or a scrap of linen which he had worn, and which from contact with his skin had become impregnated with his personality. Portions of these were incorporated with the wax of a doll which they modelled and clothed to resemble their victim. Thenceforward all the inflictions to which the image was subjected were experienced by the original; he was consumed with fever when his effigy was exposed to the fire, he was wounded when the figure was pierced with a knife. The Pharaohs themselves had no immunity from these spells." Nor need we go back as far as the Pharaohs to find witches and wizards making use of effigies for the undoing of their enemies. According to Mr. Elworthy, from whose interesting book on the "Evil Eye" I have already quoted, such images and figures were used in quite modern times by "witches" among the Somersetshire peasants, and dried pigs' and sheeps' hearts studded with pins have been found in old cottages in that county dedicated to the same malevolent purpose. Onions were also sometimes used in the same way. A lady, who lived many years in a rural parish of Somerset, also told me only a few months ago that she had there known several people who were supposed to be witches, and had seen hanging in their chimneys, dried animals' hearts, stuck full of pins, intended to injure their own or other people's enemies.

A well-known "white witch" lives and flourishes to-day in the village of T——n, in South Pembrokeshire. Some most interesting particulars concerning her were sent me a few weeks ago, by a correspondent in that county. My friend wrote: "An old man, David Evans, (no relation to the witch) . . . who has worked . . . for thirty years, 'failed,' as they say in Pembrokeshire, some time ago, and has done

N

no work for seventeen weeks. He has had medical advice and medicine, but with no satisfactory results. . . . He took it into his head that he would consult the 'charmer.' I was on my way to visit him and his wife, when I met Mr. Blank's bailiff, Pike, who told me he had sent him to T——n that very day, and that I should only find the wife at home. . . . When I got to the house I found the old man had returned. . . . He told me whom he had been to see, and I naturally wanted to know all about it. The following is what he told me:

" ' When I got to Gwen Davies' * house, I told her about myself, and how long I had been ill, and that I had seen the doctor and had bottles of physic and was no better. She made me sit down in a chair and she laid eleven little pieces of straw on the table ; then she took a long straw and waved it several times round my head; having done this she went to the table and removed one of the little bits of straw to another part of the table. When this was done she came back to me and repeated the waving of the long straw, and so on till all the eleven little bits of straw had been removed from where they had been put at the beginning.'

" I asked whether the 'charmer' had said anything during this performance. 'She mumbled something each time she was at the table, but I could not make out the words.'

* The witch's name and that of her patient are of course changed.

"I inquired then, 'What did she say to you when this was over?'

"David Evans replied that she said that he would recover, but that it would be a long time. . . .

"'What advice did she give you as to what you should eat, drink, and avoid?'

"'Eat all you can get,' she told him, 'but no doctor's stuff, and no drink.' My last inquiry was, 'Did you give her anything?'

"'No,' said the old man, 'she would take nothing.' I think I may safely say this is a properly authenticated narrative."

To this account my friend a few days later added the following postscript.

"To add something to my last letter. I met our Archdeacon . . . on Friday, and was telling him about the 'White Witch of T——n'; he had heard of her when he was Vicar of L——n; his account of her proceedings is slightly different from what I wrote to you;— the little bits of straw are more than eleven, and she moves them, not on a table, but on two chairs, transferring them from one to the other; and what the old man described as 'mumbling' is that she repeats passages from the Bible. This latter fact connects, in my mind, her 'hanky-panky' with the old ceremony of 'touching' for the King's Evil."

The slight discrepancy in the details of the witch's proceedings in nowise detracts from the central, most interesting fact, that such professional "charmers" should be still resorted to in the rural districts of Wales by invalids having apparently every faith in their ability to work cures.

It was the Rector of Llaw——n who kindly gave me many particulars of a very famous "wise man" known as Harries of Caio. These are real names ; Caio is a parish in Carmarthenshire, and my clerical friend had formerly been Vicar there, though subsequent to Harries' death, which occurred some years ago. But he is well remembered and talked of in the country, and if all tales told of him are true he must have possessed considerable psychic powers, which in these days would by no means be thought supernatural by enlightened people, but which thirty or forty years ago would most certainly have impressed and awed an ignorant peasantry. Harries is described as a fine-looking man with a long beard and remarkably bushy eyebrows. He would occasionally tramp the country, carrying an enormous volume of astrological lore under his arm, leather-bound, with a strong lock attached. This, he said, was to prevent ignorant people reading the charms contained in the book, and thereby raising evil spirits.

Although often consulted as a healer it was on his powers as a seer or prophet that Harries' fame chiefly rested. If any one had a relation ill or in trouble, he would go to the wizard and ask what his friend's fate would be. Harries then put himself into a trance, and when he came out of it would say, " I am sorry for you,

but your friend will die," or " he will recover,"
as the case might be.

But the most interesting story connected
with Harries of Caio, and one which the Rector
of Llaw——n had heard on excellent authority,
is as follows : A certain man in Carmarthenshire started one day to walk over the hills to
Breconshire on some farming business. He did
not return when expected; time went by, and
his friends became alarmed and made inquiries,
but to no purpose ; nothing could be heard
about him. At last the police were called in,
but they were equally unsuccessful, and after
many weeks had passed without news of the
missing man, his relations determined as a last
resource to apply to the wizard of Caio. So a
deputation of them went to his house, and
having stated the purpose of their visit were
told by Harries that he could give them the
information they sought. " But," he added
solemnly and with great feeling, "I am sorry
to tell you that your friend is no longer alive.
If you cross the mountain between Llandovery
and Brecon your path will lead you past a
ruined house, and near that house there is a
large and solitary tree. Dig at the foot of
that tree and you will find him whom you seek."
These words of gloomy import only crystallised
the feelings of vague foreboding already in the
minds of the inquirers, who, after a short consultation, determined to test the truth of the
wizard's information. A small party was
formed, who proceeded, according to the seer's

directions, along the lonely track that led over the mountain to Brecon, the way by which it was known their friend had intended to travel. After a while they came to a ruined cottage, with a large tree close by—landmarks probably known to most of them. Dead leaves covered the ground beneath the tree, but on raking these aside it was at once seen that the earth had been lately disturbed, and on digging deep below Harries' words were sadly verified. by the searchers, who did indeed discover the body of their friend. That a crime had been committed was abundantly clear, but by whom has remained a mystery to this day, nor was any ordinary explanation ever sufficient to account for Harries' extraordinary information on the subject, all inquiry—and also his high character—precluding the most remote suspicion of his being in any way connected with such a misdeed.

After Harries' death his " magic books" were sold, and are now in the possession of the Registrar of the Welsh University College at Aberystwith.

Mention of Llandovery reminds me of a celebrated " Curse story " connected with Cardiganshire, but which has been so often the theme of abler pens than mine that I shall do little more than refer to it here. Briefly it is this. In the seventeenth century, Maesyfelin Hall, a large house some few miles from Lampeter, was the centre of hospitality and culture in Cardiganshire. Judge Marmaduke Lloyd, owner of the house and great estates, was universally known and respected in South Wales, counting among his intimate friends the well-known Vicar Pritchard of Llandovery, whose book, "Canwyll y Cymru" (The Welshman's Candle), is still much prized for its quaintly pious teaching by all religious Welsh people. This clergyman had a son, Samuel, who seems to have been a frequent and welcome visitor at Maesyfelin, until a day came when a terrible tragedy occurred. The young man's body, bearing evidence that he had been foully done to death, was found floating in the river Teify, and dark must have been the suspicions of his grief-stricken parent when he could pen words such as the following, fraught with deadly enmity towards his former friends :

> "The curse of God on Maesyfelin fall,
> On root of every tree, on stone of wall,
> Because the flower of fair Llandovery town,
> Was headlong cast in Teivi's flood to drown."

Or in the original Welsh :

> "Melldith Duw ar Maesyfelin
> Ar bob carreg, dan bob gwreiddyn,
> Am daflu blodeu tref Llandyfri
> Ar ei ben i Deifi i foddi."

Tradition asserts that Samuel Pritchard met his death in some brawl arising from the discovery of his persistence in some prohibited love affair ; but the whole story rests on the most slender evidence, and beyond the fact that he lost his life by violence, somewhere between Lampeter and Llandovery, there is nothing to prove that the family of Maesyfelin had any share at all in the dark deed. However, not many generations passed before it seemed as if the Vicar's words had indeed taken effect, for after Sir Marmaduke's death, the estate of Maesyfelin was gradually weakened by the extravagance of his descendants, and finally what was left of the land passed through marriage into the possession of the Lloyds of Peterwell in the year 1750. Maesyfelin Hall was left empty, and time and neglect have most literally fulfilled to the letter the curse pronounced by Vicar Pritchard nearly three hundred years ago. Not an unusual history, and one that might probably be true of many an old and extinct family in Great Britain. But in Cardiganshire the reverses and final extinction of the Lloyds of Maesyfelin were always ascribed to the effect of the pious. Vicar's malison. Oddly enough, that curse seemed to follow the name of Lloyd, for the family of Peterwell had no better luck with the Maesyfelin estates than the original owners. At the death of John Lloyd of Peterwell, his great property, including Maesyfelin, went to his brother Herbert, who was made a baronet in 1763, and sat in Parliament for seven years. He was a man of extravagant tastes and imperious temper, and seems to have ruled like a dictator in his own neighbourhood. Many and interesting are the tales still told of him and his ways, and the manner of his death and burial were as sensational as his career through life might lead one to expect. But all that is "another story," and here it is sufficient to say that, Sir Herbert Lloyd dying deeply in debt and without descendants, his heavily mortgaged lands passed to strangers and were divided, while his great house of Peterwell, with its "four gilded domes," became, like Maesyfelin, a ruin, of which only the broken walls remain to tell of former splendours. And the famous curse, having fulfilled its end, is now forgotten, or remembered in the district only as an interesting tradition.

A Scotch friend once told me of a curse that had been laid upon her own family by three Highlanders. These men were implicated in the '45 Rebellion, and were handed over to the Duke of Cumberland by an ancestor of my friend, a man whose sympathies were Hanoverian, and the owner of considerable property. The Highlanders were duly condemned and executed, but before they died they solemnly cursed their enemy, prophesying that his descendants in the third generation should not possess an acre of land. This prophecy was fulfilled to the letter; and my friend tells me that a relation of hers has talked with a very old woman who came from the same part of the country, and who spoke of the curse and its origin as well-known facts.

Connected with this subject of family curses

is a story I heard not long ago, of a certain
country house in one of the Eastern Counties.
On the landing of the principal staircase of this
house there might be seen, a few years since, a
glass case covered by a curtain, which, if drawn,
revealed the waxen effigy of a child, terribly
wasted and emaciated, lying on her side as if
asleep. It was described to me as so realistic
as to be quite horrible, and it is apparent that
some very strong reason must have existed for
keeping so unpleasant an object in such a
thoroughfare of the house. Its history is this.
Some generations ago, the wife of the owner of
the place died, leaving motherless a little girl.
The father soon married again, giving his child
a cruel stepmother, who, in her husband's
absence from home, so ill-treated and starved
the poor little girl that very soon after her
father's return she died. It is said that the
facts of his wife's cruelty reached the father's
ears, and in order that he might punish her
with perpetual remorse, he had a wax model
made of his child exactly as she appeared in
death, and placed it conspicuously on the staircase landing, where his wife must see it whenever she went up or down stairs. He further
directed in his will that the model should
never be removed from its place, adding that if
it were, *a curse* should fall on house and family.
So, covered in later years by a curtain, the
effigy remained until a day arrived in quite
recent times, when the family then in possession
were giving a dance, and for some reason had

the case containing the wax-work carried downstairs and put in an outhouse. But mark what happened. That very night occurred a shock of earthquake violent enough to cause part of the house to fall down! Very likely mere coincidence; but as it *might* have been the working of the curse consequent on the removal of the case, it was thought advisable to restore the grisly relic to its former position, where, as far as my informant knew, it may be seen to this day.

CHAPTER IX

ODD NOTES

> " Plain and more plain, the unsubstantial Sprite
> To his astonish'd gaze each moment grew ;
> Ghastly and gaunt, it reared its shadowy height,
> Of more than mortal seeming to the view,
> And round its long, thin, bony fingers drew
> A tatter'd winding-sheet, of course *all white*."

IN that very interesting book, "John Silence," Mr. Algernon Blackwood remarks that cats seem to possess a peculiar affinity for the Unknown, and that while dogs are invariably terrified by anything in the nature of occult phenomena, cats, on the contrary, are soothed and pleased.

Perhaps that is why cats have so often figured in history and fiction as companions of sorcerers and witches ; and perhaps it was a knowledge of their occult sympathies that helped to render these animals sacred to the ancient Egyptians. These are only speculations, but there is no doubt that cats are, in fact, queer and sphinx-like creatures ; capable moreover of inspiring an extraordinary dread and dislike (quite out of proportion to their size and character) in some people. It is said that Lord Roberts, bravest of Generals, cannot stand the sight of a cat. I have known personally at least two people who have the same loathing and fear; and one of these individuals can tell if a cat is anywhere near without either seeing or hearing it; and I have seen this exemplified when my friend has been assured—in good faith—that there was not a cat in the house, much less in the room. But on search being made a cat was found—though no one knew how it got there. And this curious instance of perception by some "sixth sense" reminds me of an odd thing I was told about a man who, until quite lately, was employed as a verger in Ely Cathedral. This man, in some unknown way, could always tell if there were any person in the Cathedral, although he could neither see, feel, nor hear them. It is said that this extraordinary faculty was tested over and over again, but the verger was never mistaken.

But to return to our friend Puss; another of her funny characteristics is, that she always seems to seek out the people who dislike her, and appears to desire their friendship, contrary to her usual habit with strangers, with whom she is generally coy and repellent. Altogether it is not difficult to credit cats with some degree of psychic power, and probably few of us would object to their comfortable Tabbies or languid Persians seeing ghosts and spirits if they are able to. But when it comes to a cat being itself a ghost, the idea is somehow horribly uncanny. Yet I know a lady who for

a long while occupied a house in Dublin where
there was a ghost cat. I had heard a vague
rumour of this, and much interested, I wrote
to Miss M——n for information. She replied
(dated October 17, 1907): "With regard to
my 'ghost cat' I have no story to tell, or
cause for its appearance. For some time my
sister and I were the only people who saw it,
but of late my niece, and also different friends
I have had staying with me, have also seen it.
It is always just walking under a table or chair
when seen, which may account for neither its
head nor front portion of its body ever having
been seen. It is coal-black. For many years
when it used to appear, I had no black cat, but
have had one now for some time, so don't
notice the ghost one so much, as we don't
bother to notice whether it is the real or the
supernatural, but know for a fact it has been
seen several times this year. I am sorry I
can't give you any further details, but not
being a believer in ghosts, I am afraid I pay
very little attention to my friendly cat."

One would like to know the *raison d'être* of
that little feline spectre, and there is doubtless
some story connected with it that would
account for its presence could we but look
back far enough into the histories of former
tenants of the house. But in a city or town,
strange happenings connected with any particular family are more quickly forgotten than
in the country, where such traditions are apt
to linger far longer in the memories of the

local inhabitants. In a town, one is told
" such and such a house is haunted "; but if
you ask why and how haunted, you will
generally meet with " I don't know " in reply.
Whereas in the country, if a house acquires a
" haunted " reputation, there is mostly chapter
and verse for its particular kind of ghost, and
often a story told to account for the haunting.

But ghostly dogs are, to my mind, quite as
unpleasant as ghostly cats, and there is something very disagreeable, I think, about the
following experience of a person whom we will
temporarily christen Mr. Archer. He was a
youngish man of strongly psychic temperament,
and in the intervals of business was accustomed
to dabble pretty freely in occult matters of all
kinds. It happened once that he went to stay
in a large northern city, where he had some
spiritualist friends, and one evening he and
these people arranged to hold a séance. Forgetting all about such a mundane affair as
dinner, they "sat" for hours, but with no
result; they could get no manifestations, and
at last gave up the attempt, Archer returning
weary and disappointed to his hotel. It was
then very late, so going to his room, he locked
the door, and proceeded to get ready for bed.
Suddenly he heard a very queer noise—a sort
of rustling and scrambling; and as he turned
quickly to see where it came from, a large,
black dog darted from under the bed. Archer
felt much annoyed at what he considered the
carelessness of the hotel servants in shutting

the animal into his room, and he promptly rushed at it with the intention of turning it out into the passage. But before he could reach it, the dog walked to the locked door and simply vanished or melted through the panels, leaving Archer in a state of bewilderment hard to describe. The incident as I heard it goes no further. But as Archer was presumably accustomed to investigating supernatural phenomena, we may suppose that he made full inquiries in the hotel as to a possible real dog, or an already known ghostly one, though apparently without satisfaction. He told the friend from whom I had the story that he had no shadow of doubt as to his having really seen the thing, and that it disappeared in the unusual manner related, and that, whatever the dog may have been, it was no hallucination. Could it have been possible, I wonder, that the fruitless séance was answerable for the creature's appearance? That not being able to raise the powers they wished, the sitters had unwittingly attracted some being from a lower plane, which Archer was able to visualise, owing to the mental effects produced by a long fast and bodily fatigue, joined to his peculiar temperament. For there is no doubt that they who deliberately set to work to " raise spirits " must take their chance of the character of such " demons " (to use the ancient name) as respond to the call.

Traditions concerning mysterious " bogies," elementals, or spirits—call them what we will

—supposed to haunt certain localities, are to be heard of in many parts of Great Britain. In Wales such legends have always abounded, and innumerable are the tales of bogies said to frequent lonely roads, and especially the neighbourhood of bridges. Many of these stories were no doubt invented for the purpose of frightening ignorant people and children, while others had their origin in the brains of intoxicated individuals returning late at night from fair or funeral. Yet it is curious how these old tales cling. There is a bridge spanning a ravine or dingle, about a mile from my own home, which had such an evil reputation for being haunted that until quite recent years no local postboy or fly-driver would take his horses over it after dark, for fear of the bogey that was said to sit on the parapet at night, or that,

" Half seen by fits, by fits half heard,"

would glide tall and menacing across the road just where the hill was steepest, and the gloom of overhanging trees most impenetrable.

Only the other day, a Merionethshire woman told me of an extraordinary apparition seen by two men whom she knew well, on the bridge in her native village. One of these men was a chapel deacon, respected and respectable, and, according to my friend, quite incapable of misrepresenting facts. Their houses were separated by the bridge, and on a certain evening, when one man had been visiting the

o

other, he said jokingly to his friend, "Now, John, you must come out and see me home, for I'm afraid to cross the bridge alone." So the two started together. It was a bright moonlight night, and arrived on the bridge, what should they see but the figure of an enormous man, clad in white, standing in the middle of the road! Remembrance of their jesting words, spoken only a few minutes before, flashed across the deacon's memory, and with their hearts in their mouths they stood rooted to the spot. But the figure, whatever it was, made no movement, and at last with shaking limbs and clammy brows, they stole past it in safety. Then came the dilemma. How was he who had acted escort to reach his own home across the bridge alone?

My informant said it was afterwards rumoured that the two friends spent the whole night escorting each other home. For neither dared ever return alone. But in fact all they themselves really said when questioned was, that they had waited what seemed to them an interminable time before the Shape which they watched vanished quite suddenly and never reappeared.

Of course this tale is capable of more than one humorous interpretation, such as that of an evening spent in overmuch good-fellowship, or as an example of a successful practical joke. But still I give it as it was told me, as an excellent instance of the Welsh " bogey

story," of a kind that might, I expect, have
been collected by the dozen in our remote
districts twenty or thirty years ago, but are
now rapidly being forgotten. I have heard
of another "bŵcgi" (as bogey becomes in
Welsh) of the same type as the above, which
used to frequent a cross-road some four miles
from Newcastle Emlyn, and took pleasure
in frightening respectable people after dark.
And still another of these creatures of the
night was supposed to haunt the grounds
of a house not far from Cardigan, and was
known as "Bŵcgi chain," its appearance
being always accompanied by the noise of
clanking chains. This bogey seems to have
been quite an institution in the neighbourhood,
and I fancy familiarity with the tradition had
bred, if not contempt, at least disregard of
poor old "Bŵcgi chain."

A friend who lives in South Cardiganshire
wrote to me of a man in her own neighbourhood—still living—who declared he had once
seen "the evil spirit" of a neighbour, "at
dawn, near a limekiln, a creature 'twixt dog
and calf, and with lolloping gait, not fierce,
but evil to look at, for the Welsh believe
that evil people can take the form of creatures
and roam about, for no good of course. And
though they never name it, and would deny
it to you or me, yet secretly, behind closed
doors, they whisper of the different forms
taken by the evil spirits of neighbours who
are workers of darkness."

Personally I have never come across this belief in Wales, but it is most likely the remains of a very ancient superstition peculiar to that district, just as the belief in the "Tanwe" (to which I alluded in a former chapter) seems to have been localised in North Cardiganshire. ·

Of course this idea of the spirit of a living person roaming about to work wickedness can be nothing more nor less than a variation of the Were-wolf or Loup-garou legend, which from time immemorial has been believed throughout almost all Europe, and, it is said, still lingers in remote parts of France, and particularly Brittany. Now, closely related in race as the Welsh are to the Bretons, it is not hard to imagine that the superstitions and beliefs of both nations have had their origin in a common stock, taking us back to those far-away times when the great Celtic tribes were young. Local circumstances, religious influences, and differences of education have combined in the course of centuries to determine the survival or decay of these old traditions in both countries, and probably the "loup-garou" ceased to be generally heard of in Wales many hundreds of years ago. But everybody who has studied even slightly the subject of folk-lore and superstition, knows how long fragments of some ancient belief (often so tattered as to be almost unrecognisable) will be found obstinately preserved in perhaps quite a small district, among a few people in whom such a belief appears as an instinct which yields but slowly before the spread of modern education. And endeavouring to follow these dwindling rivulets of strange old-world ideas to their source is one of the most fascinating subjects of speculation in the world.

However, all this is digression, and we must come back to our Welsh bogies, for to omit mention of the Gŵrach or Cyhoeraeth, which is the most terrible of them all, would be unpardonable. Fortunately, to see or hear one of these spectres seems to be very rare. Howells, in his " Cambrian Superstitions," says that the Cyhoeraeth is a being with dishevelled hair, long black teeth, lank withered arms, a frightful voice, and cadaverous appearance. "Its shriek is described as having such an effect as literally to freeze the blood in the veins of those who heard it, and was never uttered except when the ghost came to a cross-road or went by some water, which she splashed with her hands . . . exclaiming 'Oh, oh fyn gŵr, fyn gŵr' (my husband, my husband), or sometimes the cry would be 'my wife, my wife,' or 'my child.' Of course this doleful plaint boded ill for the relations of those who were unlucky enough to hear it, and if the cry were merely an inarticulate scream it was supposed to mean the hearer's own death."

The wailing cry of the Welsh Cyhoeraeth reminds one of the Irish banshee legends; and though I have never so far come across any one who has seen or heard the Cyhoeraeth, yet two people in Wales have told me of death warnings conveyed by what they called " banshees."

One story concerns a Welsh lady, Miss W——, who happened to be staying at an hotel at Bangor, in North Wales, and was awakened one night by a hideous, wailing cry. Much alarmed, she got up, and as she reached the window (from whence the sound came) saw slowly and distinctly cross it the shadow of some great flying creature, while the dreadful cry died gradually away. Miss W—— felt half frozen with fear, but managed to open the window and look into the street. Nothing was to be seen ; but afterwards, as she lay awake, trying to account for what she had seen and heard, a possible, though perhaps far-fetched solution, occurred to her.

Next morning, when breakfasting, she asked the waiter whether he knew if any Irish person in the house or street had died. The man looked rather surprised at the question, and said " No." Presently, however, he came hurrying back to Miss W—— and said " Colonel F.," mentioning a well-known name, " a gentleman from Ireland, who has been staying here very ill for some time, died last night."

Miss W—— was always firmly convinced that what she heard and saw that night at Bangor were the shadow and the warning cry of the Colonel's family banshee.

The other instance was told me by a friend, who declared that being awakened one night when staying in the town of Cardigan by an extraordinary and startling noise at his window, he jumped up, threw open the window and looked out. And there, *flying* down the street he saw what he called "a banshee"-like spectre "of horror indescribable, which beat its way slowly past the silent houses till it disappeared in the gloom beyond. It returned no more, and the rest of the night passed undisturbed; but on receiving unexpected news next day of the death of a great friend, my informant could not help thinking of the extraordinary incident, and wondering if the "banshee" had brought a warning.

It is a common belief in Wales that the screeching of barn-owls close to a house is a very bad sign, betokening the approach of death, and certainly it requires no great effort of the imagination to produce a shudder of foreboding as the gloom of an autumn evening is suddenly rent by the weird cry. And though I am no believer in what is of course a mere superstition, yet the recollection of it came to my mind on an occasion when I happened to be staying at a country house where a death occurred somewhat unexpectedly. I well remember the incessant and extraordinary noise made by the owls during a few evenings immediately before and after the event, shriek following shriek, often appearing to be just outside the windows; and though every one

knew it was only the owls, yet it would be
difficult to describe the uncanny, disturbing
effect produced on one's mind by such an
unearthly-sounding clamour. This was only
coincidence; but whether regarded as prophetic
or not, the "gloom-bird's hated screech," as
Keats calls it, is not a cheerful sound, and
seems a fitting accompaniment to that hour

> " In the dead vast and middle of the night
> When churchyards yawn."

Mysterious knockings and taps, or the sound
of an invisible horse's hoofs stopping at the
door, are also thought in Wales to be death
omens. It is said that in the old days of lead-
mining in Cardiganshire, the miners always
used to declare that to hear "the knockers"
at work was "a sure sign" of an accident
coming.

I once heard a story about a woman belonging
to a parish not far from my own home, who
went with her husband to live in Glamorganshire, where he heard of work at Pontypridd,
to which town he betook himself, leaving his
wife at Dowlais. But a terrible accident
happened in the mine where the man worked,
and he was killed. His body was brought
back to his wife's house at Dowlais, and as the
coffin was carried into one of the upstairs rooms,
it was carelessly allowed to knock noisily
against the door. The widow afterwards told
her friends that two nights before the accident
happened she had been awakened in that very

room, by a loud sound exactly like that caused by the bumping of the coffin, and could not imagine what had made such an odd noise. She was thenceforward convinced that a premonitory sound of the coffin being carried into the room had been sent her as a "warning."

There is a house I know very well in South Wales where a curious sound, always supposed to be of "ghostly" origin, used to be heard occasionally by a lady who lived there for a few years. She described it as the noise "of a person digging a grave," or using a pick-axe for that purpose, and said it was most horrible and gruesome to hear. It appeared to come from just outside the drawing-room windows, yet nothing was to be seen if one looked out. Other tenants have come and gone since that lady's time, and I have never heard again of the ghostly grave-digger. But mysterious footsteps have been heard in that house quite lately, and by three people who say they do not "believe in ghosts"; one of them, however, admitted to me that in spite of close investigation he was utterly unable to account for the soft footfalls he most certainly heard. But it may well be that invisible presences still linger about a place which in olden times was the site of a little settlement of monks, though nothing now remains but the name to remind us of the fact.*

* There is a tradition connected with this house concerning a former owner who was a miser and died about a century ago, to the effect that his spirit is imprisoned

While on the subject of warnings and death
omens, I may mention a curious tradition
connected with an old church I know in
Pembrokeshire. In a corner of the building is
kept the bier used at funerals; and it is
reported that always just before any death
occurs in the parish, this bier is heard to creak
loudly, as though a heavy burden had been
laid upon it. The churchyard adjoining has
also a haunted reputation, and I have been
told that not even a tramp would willingly
pass its gates after dark.

Another death warning is the tolling—by
unseen hands—of the bell of Blaenporth Church
(in Cardiganshire). This eerie sound was said
to be always heard at midday and midnight
just before the death of any parishioner of
importance. But as far as I can gather, the
Blaenporth bell has ceased to toll its warnings;
for an inhabitant of the parish, who knows the
country people and their ideas very well, told
me she had never heard of the mysterious
tolling, and thought it must be a dead tradition. But it is a picturesque one, and so
characteristic of Celtic ideas, ever interpreting
as signs and portents the slightest incident
that happens to break the ordinary routine
of life, that I thought it worth recording
here.

Another superstition (certainly not pictu-

within a certain rock on the coast about two miles away,
where he is doomed to stay until he has picked his way
out with a pin!

resque), which I have never heard of but in Cardiganshire, was that it was very unlucky to bury the bodies of any cattle that happened to be found dead in the fields! What idea can have been connected with such an unsanitary prejudice I cannot imagine.

When reading a paper at a local antiquarian meeting some few weeks ago, the Vicar of Lledrod,* Mr. H. M. Williams, referred to the origin of the Welsh word " Croesaw," which means "welcome"; and in explanation he related how he came to realise that the word was derived from the noun *croes* (a cross). He said : " A farmer's wife, whenever I visited her house, as soon as she saw me at the door, would take some instrument of iron, such as a poker or knitting-needle, and cere- moniously describe a cross on the hearth, and would afterwards address me with the words ' Croesaw i' chwi, syr.' (' Welcome to you, sir.') This custom existed at Llanddeusant, Carmarthenshire, where I lived twenty years ago."

This strikes me as one of the most curious survivals of an ancient superstition that I have heard of in Wales. Of course there can be no doubt as to the word " croesaw " being derived from the " croes " made as described above ; but the question is, why was that cross made at all ? The Vicar, who is a scholar and learned antiquary, and whose views should therefore be regarded with respect, seemed to think that

* A Cardiganshire parish.

the cross was a sort of sign and seal of
welcome, as a man in old days would set his
mark—a cross—to anything as a signification
of approval and affirmation. Perhaps that is
so; but my own idea (advanced with all
diffidence) is that the cross had a far different
meaning, and that it had its origin in the
mediæval dread of the "evil eye." A stranger
coming to the house must ever be welcomed
according to the laws of Welsh hospitality,
and he might very likely be quite guiltless of
the uncanny power to "ill-wish" or "overlook." But to avoid risks, it was better to use
some simple charm, before bidding the visitor
enter, and what could be more powerful against
malign influences than the holy symbol of the
cross quickly made in the ashes, where it could
be as easily obliterated the next moment, and
so wound nobody's feelings. Again, the use of
the poker or knitting-needle for the rite seems
to be a remnant of the old universal belief that
witches, evil spirits, and ghosts hated iron, and
cannot harm a person protected by that metal.
Such at least is my explanation of a most
interesting local custom, which has become
mechanical nowadays—just as many of us cross
ourselves when we see a magpie, without
knowing why—and perhaps by this time has
disappeared altogether.

Mr. Williams tells me he has never met
with this custom in Cardiganshire, but says
that a curious little ceremony used to be performed, about fifty years ago, by the children

of the parish of Verwig, near Cardigan. " As
the children were going home from school, at
a cross-road before parting, one of the elder
ones would describe a cross on the road and
solemnly utter the following holy wish :

"Gris Groes,"
"Myn Un, ie, Myn Un, aed mys moes."

Rendered in English this is:

" Christ's Cross
By the Holy One, yea by the Holy One, may gentle
manners prevail."

What the quaint little ceremony meant it is
hard to say, and no doubt the children themselves could have given no reason for its
performance, except that " they always did
it." But it was a pretty idea, whatever its
esoteric meaning, which would probably lead
us back to the days when Wales was Roman
Catholic, and nearly all instruction, both as
regards book-learning and manners, in the
hands of priests and monks. Then it is
not difficult to imagine some such simple
charm or invocation taught his wild scholars
by the gentle schoolmaster-monk of the local
monastery, to help carry the peace of the
cloister home with them, and as a safeguard
against the emissaries of Satan, in whose
active power to work ill our forefathers so
firmly believed. And it may be that the
slight element of mystery—always attractive

to childish minds—connected with the making of the cross may have helped to preserve the little custom, when one dependent on words alone would more readily have been forgotten.

CHAPTER X

CONCLUSION

> " The wind-borne mirroring Soul :
> A thousand glimpses wins,
> And never sees a whole."

IT is easier to write the title of this chapter
than its contents. For what general conclusion can be satisfactory, regarding all these
instances of the supernatural? Every one has
his own ideas about them, ranging from the
sceptic's point of view to that of the most
credulous believer, both attitudes of mind to
be equally deprecated when dealing with
occult phenomena. However, such extremes
of opinion are becoming rare, while the number
of people who preserve an open mind on such
subjects is ever increasing, and this, I venture
to think, is the right way of regarding "the
Unknown." For blind negation has never
enlightened any one, while uncritical acceptance of unsubstantiated statements is equally
prejudicial to real knowledge. Of course, this
attitude of toleration, and, as it were, awaiting
further revelation, is essentially a modern one.
Our forefathers of three or four hundred years
ago would have thought us poor creatures for

holding our judgment in suspense. Most
people then believed in "ghosts" and held
it no shame to do so; while the minority of
the superior who disbelieved took no pains
to dissemble their scorn and contempt for
those who did. There was never any attempt
at impartial investigation of supernatural occurrences; one section would have had neither
the courage nor intelligence necessary, while
the other would have scorned the undertaking.
So Superstition's sway remained unchecked
for many a long century, and though its power
began to dwindle directly education became
a systematic affair amongst civilised nations,
yet it is only in recent years that one has
begun to foresee a time when its terrors will
have disappeared for good and all. Because it
is only within the last few decades that men
of great and trained intellect have discovered
that the methods of science and law apply
as perfectly in the investigation of psychic as
in material phenomena; and that discovery
once made, I cannot help thinking that it is
merely a matter of time before mankind
penetrates the mystery of the Unseen, though,
as I have said before, this will not happen in
our generation. At present we are only at
the beginnings of things; learning the alphabet
of a whole new series of experiences, one of
which is telepathy, or thought communicating
thought, without aid of the ordinary senses.
We know this wonderful power does exist,
reliable experiment has proved it, but so far

we know little more, and can only guess that some minds in some way—probably unknown to themselves—possess the mysterious faculty of setting in motion vibrations that travel along a medium finer and rarer far than the famous Hertzian waves. But presently the laws that govern such vibrations will be discovered, and mind will then speak to mind at will, even across half the world. And telepathy, which we are still apt to think of as something almost supernatural, will then be as much a matter of course as wireless telegraphy is in our day.

However, at present we are only on the threshold of these marvels, and we who are not engaged in the task of occult discovery can still be interested and entertained by " ghost stories " *as* ghost stories, and can discuss various points and form our own ideas about them. And there is one feature common to a great many of these supernatural tales and incidents which I think must strike everybody, whether believers or sceptics, and that is their apparent lack of purpose. There are, as we have seen, ghostly happenings which come as " warnings," though, as I have remarked in a former chapter, these warnings seldom appear to avert disaster. But in nine cases out of ten odd things are seen or heard, and nothing particular happens afterwards. The question— and a puzzling one—is, why should these things occur at all ? Why should such a tremendous reversal of the laws which ordinarily

govern our human environment take place, as
is implied by, let us say, the extraordinary
experience of Miss Travers at Glanwern, related in Chapter III.? Of course in this
volume I have tried to collect ghost stories
that *did* mean something, as naturally they
are the more interesting type of incident. But
I have heard innumerable instances of people
hearing and seeing strange things, followed by
no particular consequences. Probably every
one knows the kind of tale, interesting to
the person concerned, but rather dull when
related.

Perhaps the following illustration will help
us to understand these inconsequent manifestations a little better. Let us imagine
ourselves as the audience in a huge, well-
lighted theatre. At least the auditorium is
lit up, but the vast stage is in complete
darkness, with a great shadowy curtain hiding
anything that may be taking place behind it
from our eyes. In fact, nobody troubles much
about the stage at all, every one is talking
and thinking of other things and few people
so much as glance towards the curtain, though
those who do dimly feel that there really is
a play going on behind it, and some of us
wish, in a vague sort of way, that we could
know what it is. But sometimes the curtain
goes up for a moment, and then, if any one
is looking, he sees a glimpse of the play; and,
not knowing what has come before or what
is to follow, it seems rather meaningless, or

even alarming. Sometimes, too, an actor will appear on the stage, or come amongst the audience with a message for one or a group of them, but only the few can see him, and his message is not always intelligible to them. Some bold people, tired of looking at the impenetrable curtain, have ventured to explore behind it, and if they escaped the dangers so braved, have tried to impart their experiences to their friends when they returned. But their accounts are often received with incredulity or lukewarm interest, some even asserting that there is really nothing at all behind the curtain, and that the explorers have merely been the victims of their own imaginations. And this they say, knowing quite well that when "carriages are called" they and every one else will have to leave the house by way of the dark stage, and be obliged to go behind the scenes and learn the mystery that the curtain hides.

In this simple illustration I have tried to convey the idea of a life—or perhaps I should rather say a Consciousness — coincident and connected with this life that we know, but separated from it by a difference of consciousness which the majority of us are not able at present to bridge. A few have done so, either by a system of mystic training, or by the natural gift of the "sixth sense," clairvoyance, second sight, whatever we like to call it, which in olden days often caused its possessors to be classed as magicians and witches. And if we grasp this idea of a consciousness, interwoven and yet by matter separated from this life, of which only a few of us can get glimpses from time to time, but which is as absolutely real, perhaps more so than the life we live here, it will help us enormously to understand the meaning of psychic phenomena, or what we call " ghost stories."   Because we shall realise that there is *continuity* behind the veil which hides the Unseen, just as there is continuity in this life, and that the law of cause and effect goes with us " behind the scenes," just as it governs our present existence.   So that we must cease to think of any supernatural incident as irrelevant or inconsequent, even if it means nothing to ourselves.   It is just a glimpse — seen " through a glass darkly "—of a life organised on lines at present unfamiliar to our own, and infused with a meaning which we cannot trace, and which we yet feel has the most intimate connection with our life here.

However, these are paths of metaphysics, in which it is not well to linger, unless one can give time and all one's thoughts to their exploration.   A little knowledge about occult matters is worse than useless ; it is absolutely dangerous, and every furlong of the road that leads to such knowledge should be marked with a red signal, for it is strewn with the wrecked intellects of those who, unequipped, have lightly followed its windings.

Regarding the chapters in this book which concern Welsh superstitions, the first idea

which occurred to me when reading them over
was the exceedingly gloomy character of these
ancient beliefs. They all seem to dwell mor-
bidly on death and its surroundings, ignoring
the lighter and happier side of life altogether.
And any one who did not know Wales might
imagine from reading these tales that the
Welsh were a sullen and silent people, given
to solitude and brooding. Nothing could be
further from the truth; they are a lively and
gregarious race and never seem to cease
talking amongst themselves. Nobody is fonder
of junketing than a Welshman or Welshwoman, nothing in the way of an outing comes
amiss; fairs, eisteddfodau, "auctions," church
and chapel festivals, political meetings, anything for a jaunt! But the most important
functions of all are—funerals. Every one goes
to a funeral, and makes it a point of honour to
do so, for the more burials you attend in your
lifetime, the greater are the number of people
who will come to your own obsequies. I often
think of the characteristic remark addressed by
a Welshwoman I knew to an English neighbour, who had no taste for gadding, and found
Cardiganshire rather *triste*. "Well indeed,
Mrs. Brown *fach*, I am sorry for you; but
indeed you should go about to fairs and
funerals, and enjoy yourself."

So as funerals and the excitement connected
with them really occupy a large place in the
minds of the Welsh country-folk, it is perhaps
not strange that superstition and folk-lore have

collected round the subject and that omens and
death warnings should be specially heeded
and repeated. Also, in spite of lively manners
and gregarious instincts, there is a curious
strain of melancholy underlying the Welsh
character, in common with the other Celtic
races; a trait which I do not think any one can
understand unless he has some Celtic blood in
his veins. It is not a melancholy which colours
the disposition, for most Welsh people are
cheerful and pleasant companions. Of course
there are variations from the type, and differences of temperament just as in other nation-
alities, but if asked suddenly to name a Welsh
characteristic, I should at once mention cheer-
fulness. And yet they are melancholy; and if
this sounds paradoxical, it cannot be helped,
because it is true. It is the primitive sadness
of an old, old race, the remembrance of

> " Old unhappy, far-off things,
> And battles long ago,"

inherited from tribal ancestors, and the days
when life was a struggle even to the strong,
and elementary passions held undisputed sway.
So it is that the Welsh character unconsciously
responds to all that touches this minor string
in its nature, and, as it were, almost enjoys
gloom and woe. This is the secret of the great
religious revivals that from time to time agitate
the Principality; the Welsh really relish their
spiritual wretchedness, and enjoy being miserable sinners (especially in company!). And

well does a revivalist like Evan Roberts understand his work, and the character of his con-
gregations, and know how to twang that minor
string. Not that I would jest at revivals; in
many cases their influence has been for per-
manent good, and the kind of people they reach
and benefit are no doubt those who require a
spiritual " dressing-down " occasionally.

Nowadays, as I have said before, belief in
corpse-candles, Toili, &c. has very much gone
out of fashion amongst the country-folk; the
present generation, having many of them been
away to London or the large towns, are much
too superior to believe such things, and it is
difficult to get the old people to talk about
them. But it is not so very long ago that
such beliefs were really part of a Welsh person's
life, and supernatural experiences only infre-
quent enough to be interesting. If John Jones
entered the village inn trembling and perspiring
declaring that he had seen the Toili—well, he
had seen it, and no one thought of questioning
his statement, but all fell to wondering " whose
Toili " it could be. And it was not only among
the lower classes that these beliefs obtained,
their " betters " often shared them. The story
is still told about here how a neighbouring
squire, head of a well-known county family,
saw the Toili in the twilight of a summer's
evening, wending its way along the road which
passed his house to the church.

The old gentleman who saw the vision has
himself been dead for over sixty years, but the

locality is probably quite unchanged from what
it must have been in his day, and I have often
thought when passing the spot how well the
natural surroundings of romantic beauty lent
themselves as a setting to any such weird
happening, and have tried to conjure up the
scene in my own mind. To this day it is said
that when a death occurs in that particular
family a corpse-light is always seen a few days
previously, flickering and quivering up the
drive from the direction of the churchyard.

But very soon all these ancient beliefs will
be obliterated in the land of Cambria; and
though it seems a pity from the picturesque
point of view, and to lovers of antiquity and
folk-lore, yet on the whole it is a good thing.
For we who are apt to bewail the passing of
the old ideas often forget that they frequently
went hand in hand with dreadful ignorance
both mental and moral. For instance, belief in
witchcraft is very interesting and picturesque
to read about in our times, but we should not
overlook the terrible consequences of it which
took the form of torturing and persecuting
hundreds of innocent persons only three hundred
years ago. Read Sir Walter Scott's " Demon-
ology and Witchcraft " if you want to know
what the result of a " picturesque superstition "
may be among ignorant people. There is no
question as to the ultimate benefit of enlighten-
ment and education, even if at first they appear
to banish originality and produce monotony of
character. But that is better than the type of

mind which could drown an old woman because she kept a black cat, and sold nasty herbal "love-philtres" to silly girls. I do not think witches were much persecuted in Wales as a matter of fact, and, as I have shown, they and "wise men" are still to be found in the country. As we have seen, superstition took other forms there, and a greater hold, because it was, I am convinced, rooted in a foundation of psychic facts, just as the "second sight" was, and I suppose is still, a fact amongst the Highlanders of Scotland. But I have no doubt that for one Welshman who did really have the vision of his own or a neighbour's funeral, there were at least ten who would make the same assertion out of their own imaginations. And probably now the real faculty is very rare indeed, for it is a gift belonging to primitive races, and ever stifled by education and self-consciousness. We cannot deplore its loss, because with it has gone a mass of darkest ignorance, but that need not prevent us from being interested in its effect on the traditions and beliefs of the country. Personally I am quite indifferent as to the amount of occult truth contained in the miscellaneous material of this volume; that some truth there is, I do not doubt, but its existence is of secondary importance in comparison with the delightful, old-world atmosphere that clings to these antiquities, and seems in some way to make us realise "the times of our forefathers" better than the history of more serious events. So let us, in

Q

our hurrying, bustling days, cherish this faint fragrance of a bygone age as long as we can; it will fade quickly enough, dying with that

"... race of yore,
Who danced their infancy upon their knee,
And told our marvelling boyhood legends store,
Of their strange ventures happed by land or sea.
How are they blotted from the things that be!
How few all weak and withered of their force,
Wait on the verge of dark eternity,
Like stranded wrecks, the tide returning hoarse,
To sweep them from our sight. . . ."

Printed in Great Britain
by Amazon

14199728R00140